SEEDS OF THE WORD

∷ Foundations series

Testifying to the faith and creativity of the Orthodox Christian Church, the Foundations series draws upon the riches of its tradition to address the modern world. These survey texts are suitable both for preliminary inquiry and deeper investigation, in the classroom or for personal study.

Peter C. Bouteneff
Series Editor

Seeds
of the Word

ORTHODOX THINKING
ON OTHER RELIGIONS

Book 2 of the Foundations series

John Garvey

ST VLADIMIR'S SEMINARY PRESS
CRESTWOOD, NEW YORK
2005

Library of Congress Cataloging-in-Publication Data

Garvey, John, 1944–
    Seeds of the Word : Orthodox thinking on other religions / John Garvey.
        p.   cm. —   (Foundations ; bk. 2)
    Includes bibliographical references.
    ISBN-13: 978-0-88141-300-7 (alk. paper)
    ISBN-10: 0-88141-300-3 (alk. paper)
    1. Christianity and other religions. 2. Orthodox Eastern Church—Doctrines.
I. Title. II. Series: Foundations (St. Vladimir's Orthodox Theological Seminary
(Crestwood, Tuckahoe, Westchester County, N.Y.)) ; bk. 2.
BR127.G37 2005
261.2—dc22

                                                        2005027219

COPYRIGHT © 2005 BY JOHN GARVEY

ST VLADIMIR'S SEMINARY PRESS
575 Scarsdale Rd, Crestwood, NY 10707
1-800-204-2665
www.svspress.com

ISSN 1556-9837
ISBN 0-88141-300-3
ISBN 978-0-88141-300-7

PRINTED IN THE UNITED STATES OF AMERICA

CONTENTS

foreword

Ours is an age where people of different faiths are likely to live side by side and have the means of communicating with others all over the globe. At the same time, especially with the rise and spread of terrorism, the faiths do not seem to be talking to each other very well. In many of today's civil and international wars, as well as in acts of terror on the part of non-national groups, the parties involved accuse the enemy of being godless infidels. In such a climate, dialogue is a critical necessity. When the rhetoric of faith becomes an inflammatory tool, the faiths involved need to begin to talk to one another. Only then, when the "other" becomes a real person, can people begin to stop generalizing and objectifying each other. At this point, they can begin to peel away stereotypes and explore the actual faith that lies behind the polemics.

When it comes to dialogue, however, we have to consider very carefully this question: What is it that we are trying to achieve? A common response is to say that we are looking for increased tolerance. But what exactly do we mean by "tolerance?" Some people take it to mean simply peaceful coexistence; others think that it means a compromise of religious convictions. In looking for a viable definition of tolerance, we need to be clear about two distinctions that are commonly overlooked:

* the difference between *tolerance* and *compromise*, and

* the difference between *firm religious belief* and *religious violence.*

If we equate tolerance with theological compromise, we will find ourselves falling into one of two camps. One rejects the pursuit of tolerance (and therefore rejects dialogue) because that process would necessarily result in yielding deeply held convictions and betraying one's faith. Another contingent embraces tolerance as compromise because this affirms their own relativist world view, where none of the world's religions can claim the truth for themselves because all are equally true. Both of these options are unacceptable.

How do we look at tolerance, then? Inter-religious dialogue is possible for the Orthodox Christian only if tolerance is taken for what it really means: *the recognition and respect of the other.* We have to believe that it is possible to co-exist with people of other faiths in a relationship of mutual respect and mutual tolerance without either side surrendering its faith convictions. To be tolerant does not mean suggesting that our own faith is wrong or lacking. In short, tolerance and compromise must be dissociated from each other.

The other commonly associated phenomena that must be consciously detached from each other are religious belief and religious violence. In fact, the reason why some people think being tolerant necessitates giving up one's convictions is precisely because they associate firm conviction with violence. They think that to believe strongly—to see certain truths as absolute or universal—necessarily means being intolerant (and by extension violent) toward persons with conflicting convictions.

When people consider faith and violence, one word that comes up often is "fundamentalism." This is a tricky word because it can refer to a specific category of Christian faith that is not by definition fanatical or small-minded.[1] But the term is now also commonly used in a pejorative sense, where "fundamentalists" are those who believe that anyone who does not share their faith is damned in the afterlife. This may also carry the assumption that a fundamentalist is ready at any time to resort to violence against people of other faiths. For again, in many people's minds, violent religious extremism is the natural extension of a firm religious belief that is unthinkingly characterized as "religious fundamentalism." This trajectory of thought is sometimes further extended: if I believe that the foundational Christian teachings are absolutely true, and therefore that contradictory teachings are false, this is *already* an act of violence. Christian apologetics become hate-speech.

This logic is highly problematic. Unless we are prepared to distinguish firmly held faith convictions from violent fundamentalism, and unless we dissociate tolerance from compromise, we are destined to choose between two "impossibles": an unacceptable isolationism and an unacceptable relativism.

---

[1] By one fairly standard definition, "Christian fundamentalism" teaches (a) the divine inspiration and inerrancy of the Scriptures, (b) Christ's virgin birth and divinity, (c) Christ's substitutionary atonement, (d) Christ's resurrection, and (e) Christ's personal pre-millennial and imminent second coming.

What we are seeking, then, is the place that admits absolute truths and absolute falsehoods, admits belief in the truth (in some cases the *exclusive* truth) of one's own faith convictions, but rejects bringing violence on people because they believe differently. We are also seeking to bring a spirit of creativity, patience, and inspired discernment to our speaking as well as to our listening—for dialogue is both.

In this volume Fr John Garvey seeks to describe just such a place. The kinds of distinctions I have described serve as his point of departure and inform the whole book. But his intention is ultimately practical. Knowing that the best way to begin considering dialogue is by informing ourselves about our dialogue partner, he devotes a substantial portion of this book to an investigation of key beliefs and practices of some of the world's major faiths. He maintains a clear and sober tone while conveying his intellectual and spiritual inquisitiveness.

Fr Garvey knows that there are a variety of ways and a variety of contexts in which Orthodox Christians have approached other faiths, ranging from missionary to polemical to apologetic. What he is seeking, and what I believe he identifies, is "a consistent Orthodox pattern" in this variegated history. Here are some of the elements of this pattern:

* The encounter between Orthodoxy and other faiths has a *long history*. Christianity since its origins has been an apologetic faith, meaning that it has had to explain itself within a pluralistic and often syncretistic context. The relationships between Christians and Jews, pagans, so-called gnostics and, later on, Muslims,

acquired different characteristics, but each was an interfaith encounter. Today, some of the most important Orthodox interfaith encounters occur in pluralistic settings, such as in the Middle East.

* The encounter between Orthodoxy and other faith is, at its best, an *informed encounter*. The earliest Christians were a minority, living under governments that often persecuted and killed them, which meant that early on, Christians had to learn to give account of themselves and their faith, if not also to persuade. But persuasion, and even self-explanation, entailed knowing the faith and presuppositions of the people being addressed.

* The encounter between Orthodoxy and other faiths *rejects relativism*. Orthodox Christians today, as in the past, have found that the most fruitful dialogues happen with partners who have deep and clear faith convictions, hold that absolute truth exists, and agree that some religious teachings are simply wrong. In such an encounter, even as one works creatively to find places of genuine and perhaps unexpected convergence, it is also necessary to name with precision the points of disagreement, to identify those positions which *cannot both be true at the same time*. Genuine dialogue cannot occur in a state of denial about real differences.

* Orthodox Christians *admit truth in other faiths*. The rejection of relativism does not mean rejecting everything in the other's faith. Indeed, the earliest Christian

apologists taught that the Word (Logos) of God, identified by Christians with Jesus Christ, is accessible in "seed form" in non-Christian and pre-Christian faiths and philosophies. Truth is truth, wherever it is found, and while Orthodox Christianity does claim uniquely to teach the fullness of truth, it does not claim a *monopoly* on truth.

∗ On that basis, Orthodox Christians are open to *mutual learning* and *mutual transformation*. This step may sound radical. But once we admit that truth exists outside our own faith, and especially if we say that everything that is true is true because it reflects Jesus Christ (who *is* the Truth), then we must be open to the ways in which God's truth has been found even in faiths that do not share our belief in Christ. Conversely, even the encounter with different, sometimes false doctrines, can shed light on our own teachings and reveal to us new dimensions of their truth. This means that while we must pray that our interfaith encounter results in a godly learning and transformation in the other, we must also pray to be open to the enrichment of our own personal faith and life.

Having identified these principles, a further problem comes to mind regarding tolerance in the inter-religious encounter: What is to be done when it is not mutual? It is one thing to work on a proper spirit of tolerance and love on our own part, but what is to be done when that spirit does not appear to be shared? What do we do, for example, with the relative *intolerance* of non-Muslims in contemporary Islamic states? There is only one answer to this question from a Christian perspective, and it is both a familiar and a hard saying: Our responsibility is to embody Christ's love and compassion, as well as his truth, in all circumstances. The receptivity of the other is not within our control and, in a way, is utterly beside the point.

This universal call to exemplify Christian love and truth and to be missionaries in Christ's name will apply differently to different people. It is not up to everyone to engage in interfaith dialogue or even in a meaningful interfaith encounter. But the imperative to reflect carefully on other faiths applies to us all. For we do live in a world where terror and intolerance, both across and within religious traditions, are very much on the rise. It is also a world in which God, in the mystery of his will, has evidently allowed a diversity of faiths to develop and flourish. And finally, as Orthodox Christianity makes its home in more and more places, situating itself increasingly in pluralistic contexts, it is essential that we consider how we ought to relate (both individually and as a Church) to other faiths and to the people who hold to them. May this book serve as a way into that reflection and as an invitation to go deeper into other faiths, as well as into our own.

—Peter C. Bouteneff

INTRODUCTION

The two views of religion that seem to prevail in our culture are contradictory. On the one hand, you encounter people who believe that religion is a completely private phenomenon, something like a matter of taste. No religious statement can be considered truer, or closer to the way things really are, than any other religious statement. All religions are equal. Religion becomes a completely subjective thing; you end up "in" one or another religion, or none, depending on how and where you were brought up.

From this relativistic point of view, no one set of values or beliefs can be seen as superior or privileged; there is no such thing as "the truth" but rather conditioned points of view. This movement away from the idea that there is such a thing as truth, and that it can be truly encountered, has permeated the popular culture. So has the sense that the main value of religion is therapeutic. It makes you feel better about yourself and provides direction in a confusing, difficult world.

The other prevailing view is broadly termed "fundamentalism." From this point of view, my religion alone has truth; anything outside my religion is false, even a work of darkness, and if you do not believe the way I believe, you will be damned for all eternity. Religious fundamentalists believe that truth can be found in one particular set of teachings and can be found clearly—it is not so much a question of struggling for clarity as accepting the truth of the given teaching. Furthermore, it is inconceivable that someone who does not hold to the one true religion might still have something to teach us or might still share in God's truth in a way that is hidden to us.

There are obviously shades of grey in between the views I have presented so simplistically, and few people will fall neatly into one or the other category. There are very sincere fundamentalists who are in practice much more tolerant than they are often seen as being, and some relativists, ironically, are downright fundamentalist in insisting that anyone who does not agree with them is a benighted fool.

How does the Orthodox Church regard other religions? That is the question explored in this book. It must be said that there are a range of approaches among Orthodox Christians. Some may sound almost relativistic; others may deny that truth can be found anywhere outside of the boundaries of the Orthodox Church. What I will try to do here is to show a consistent Orthodox pattern in dealing with other religions, drawing on theology, history, and present-day experience.

Orthodoxy has, from the start, dealt with other religions, the first of which were the religions of the world into which it was born: Judaism, which was the earliest Christian context, and the pagan religions and philosophies with which it first had to contend.

In confronting these religions, there is an Orthodox tradition that can be traced back to the beginning of the Church's history, and it engages what might seem two contradictory claims:

* Orthodoxy insists that the fullness of truth is found in Orthodoxy. The Orthodox Church understands itself to be the Apostolic Church and affirms that no other Church, religion, or philosophy can show forth that fullness in quite the same way, or so completely.

* At the same time, Orthodox have believed from the earliest years of the Church's history that God has worked outside the boundaries of the Church and that religious truths have been manifested in other places. In its missionary work, Orthodoxy has at times been able to bless traditions that originated outside of Christianity because they not only did not contradict Christian belief but also in some ways were consistent with it and, therefore, should be received.

The second claim stands to reason, because it is unlikely that God would make the right path so completely obscure that only one tradition could see it at all, and all the others would be completely lost. We often encounter people who reject all religion because religions say so many different and contradictory things, and all claim to be the true way. But these people must not have looked closely at many serious religious traditions because what is more remarkable than their contradictions is their agreement. At the end of *The Abolition of Man,* the great Christian writer C. S. Lewis offers a selection of readings from a number of religious and philosophical traditions, showing how Taoism, Christianity, Buddhism, Judaism, Islam, and Greek philosophy agree on many ethical and spiritual principles.

Orthodox Christians take this point seriously and celebrate it. But they do not join with those who say, because of this agreement on so many profound and important points, "All religions are finally the same. We are all climbing the mountain, reaching the same peak by different routes." This is an attractive idea on its surface, especially in a world which has been torn apart by so many religious wars. But, as we shall see, it ultimately takes none of the great traditions seriously, on their own terms.

The differences matter at least as much as the similarities, and the differences teach and challenge us to understand our own tradition more deeply. The way Buddhists understand the self conflicts with the Christian understanding in interesting and illuminating ways. The horror Jews and Muslims feel at the thought that the God who is Lord of the universe could have taken on human flesh, becoming "like us in all things but sin," challenges us to see that if we are wrong about this central proclamation of our faith, we really are blasphemers. The fact that some others may be so shocked by the central revelation of Christianity might startle us into seeing how radical the claims of Christianity are, and we would not encounter it if we refused to take other religions seriously enough to listen deeply to what they have to say. As we will see, the history of Judaism and Christianity has shown that the Christian tradition can absorb truths from other religions and grow from that contact.

So, a dialogue is necessary and can help us to sharpen our appreciation of our own Orthodox heritage. But, we do have to insist on a few things that make some people uncomfortable. We cannot, finally, be relativists. We must affirm that Jesus Christ is the Word of God who became human for the redemption of all human beings. Among some Christians today this truth is sometimes muted, or even denied. Jesus is the way for us, they say, but not necessarily the redemptive truth for Jews, or Buddhists, or Muslims; they have their own ways. This is not the Orthodox view.

We have to say that if Jesus was not the redeemer of all human beings, then he redeemed no one. The gospel is for all human beings. It is sometimes said that Orthodox Christians do not proselytize, and if that means that we do not apply coercive pressure on people to join us—that is true—or it should be. But it is our duty as Christians to let others know what we believe to be a matter of life or death and leave them free to respond. Here we must take some personal responsibility: it is one thing to preach the gospel and another to live it. When our lives contradict what we preach, we should not be surprised that those to whom we preach are not impressed by what we say.

We do not know, or claim to know, God's will for those who do not accept the gospel, except to say that God is a merciful and loving God who draws all people toward eternal life, and we can leave it to God to do that, in God's own way. But we are obliged to bear witness to the gospel by living it and by preaching it.

In this book, we will begin by looking at several of the world's great religions, giving them each a chance to speak, and then we will turn to look at the way the Orthodox Church has historically encountered other religions. We will examine some modern Orthodox approaches to mission work and inter-religious dialogue—especially important since, during the last several centuries, Orthodoxy has moved into the Americas, Africa, and Asia, in the process encountering a new religious frontier. Looking also at how other Christians have explored the question of dialogue between major religious traditions, we will then return to the religions we examined in order to look for some of the more relevant and useful points for interfaith discussion.

One final word of caution: Many people who undertake the study of comparative religion find that there is a natural impulse, when you see something that resembles your own belief in another context, to say, "This is what makes us like them, or them like us." For example, Buddhism speaks often about compassion, and a Christian might be inclined to overvalue this, to see it as more central to Buddhism than it may in fact be. This is not to deny its importance in Buddhism, but it is not as important as the enlightenment that leads to compassion. Similarly, we may be impressed by the Muslim devotion to Jesus, but this is not the Jesus Christians worship. This Jesus is not the incarnate Son of God, he was not crucified for our sins, nor does his suffering join with ours; indeed, the Muslim Jesus was not crucified.

The differences between religious traditions are sometimes obvious and sometimes subtle, but they matter deeply. At various points we will note similarities between, for example, aspects of Orthodox theology and the theologies of other religions, but they are not absolute similarities, and, if taken too quickly to heart, they can be deceiving. As someone said once about the North and South poles, they look the same in some places, but between them is all the difference in the world. We may learn from what Buddhists say about compassion, and we may learn some things we would never otherwise have known. We should be grateful for this, without too easily equating things that need to be seen discretely and in context.

chapter one

THE MONOTHEISTIC
TRADITION

T here is a certain ambivalence about the term "other religions." Here it does not mean other Christian traditions, such as Roman Catholicism and the various forms of Protestantism. What we mean are the non-Christian religions, ranging from the other forms of monotheism to religions that are not theistic (meaning that the idea of a creator God is not at their center and in some cases not even part of the picture). There are good reasons for us to know what they teach because in a world with increasingly porous borders we are likely to have people who share these beliefs as our neighbors. If we try to speak to a Buddhist about what he or she believes, assuming that Buddha is the god of the Buddhists, we will be mistaken. We will also be mistaken if, when talking with a Muslim, we believe that Allah is a God other than the one we worship (albeit in a radically different way). We cannot expect others to understand what we mean when we speak of Jesus as divine, if we cannot hear or understand what they believe.

What I will offer here is a brief presentation of the broadest categories of religious belief, followed by summaries of the major teachings of a number of non-Christian religions. There will be no polemic here, no attempt to show "where they go wrong." The differences between their teachings and Christianity are apparent enough, and the point is not to win a debate but to understand the foundation of the other religion's beliefs.

Many accounts of religion proceed historically, beginning with the most ancient and proceeding toward the most recent, so that, for example, you might begin with Zoroastrianism or Hinduism and move forward in time. Here we will begin with the monotheistic religions and then look at Asian religions. While there is a great deal of misunderstanding among monotheists—Christians, Muslims, and Jews—there is also a great deal of common ground between them, and a discussion of the differences may illuminate what they have in common that is not shared with Hinduism or Buddhism.

At the same time, we have something to learn from those whose religious traditions emphasize the transformation of the self through striving and effort, as Asian religions do. It is remarkable, for example, that much of what Buddhist writing has to say about mindfulness in meditation is echoed in the *Philokalia* and other Orthodox writing. This does not mean that it is, in the end, all the same—it definitely is not, and some of the deep differences will become apparent in the summaries of belief that follow. But it does show that what St Justin referred to as "seeds of the Word"[1] can be found far from home. And, even when speaking of Asian religions as having to do with the transformation that comes through striving and effort, we have to be careful. The Pure

---

[1]*Second Apology*, 13.

Land tradition within Buddhism comes very close to a Christian understanding of grace, as does the *bhakti* tradition in Hinduism.

We can see these seeds of the Word as a sign that there is something inchoate, inarticulate in the human spirit that longs for an expression, comes close, and is finally given voice in the Gospels, in the revelation of the incarnate Word of God. This is not the same thing as speaking of religion in all of its forms as "Humanity's search for God." As C. S. Lewis pointed out, this is a little like speaking of the mouse's search for the cat. Monotheism has emphasized this aspect of God—the God who reveals himself even as he hides himself—and that is where we will begin.

MONOTHEISM

The three major monotheistic religions are Judaism, Christianity, and Islam. Other religions have monotheistic beliefs—the Sikhs are monotheists, but this is largely due to Islamic influence, and some Hindus say that they are monotheists, seeing one God under many forms—but to the extent that they speak in terms of one God, it may be said that this has been the result of an encounter with Judaism, Christianity, or Islam.

The ancient world was for the most part polytheistic, and the Greco-Roman approach to the gods was pragmatic. Gods were to be used for human advantage. A soldier might sacrifice to Ares or Mars, the god of war; a wine-maker to Bacchus, the god of the grape and wine; a scholar to Athena—all to gain advantage. Some gods, such as Dionysius, were associated with ecstatic experience and the extremes of desire and longing; others, such as Apollo, were associated with order and reason. All could be named, all had a purpose, and all reflected human experience in various ways, so that what modern atheists have said of God—that "Man made God in his image and likeness"—could fairly be translated into "Ancient humans worshipped gods made in their image and likeness." A god who could not be of advantage to you was no kind of god at all. There was a kind of hedging of bets: one shrine that Paul noted in Athens (see Acts 17.23) was dedicated "to an unknown god." Paul tried to use this as a preaching point, saying "what you worship as unknown I am going to proclaim to you," but the shrine was probably placed there for someone who was scrupulous enough to make sure that he had covered all his bases.

Judaism

The God of the Jews was radically different from the other ancient gods. Some scholars have argued that Judaism was originally polytheistic and evolved into a monotheistic faith. They cite the fact that one of the Hebrew words translated as "God" is "elohim," a plural form. The language of some parts of the Bible suggests that the God of the Jews was the greatest god, that they were to worship no other, but it does not deny the reality of other gods (see 1 Cor 8.5–6). Whatever the ancient origins of Israel's belief may be, a certainty grew among the Jews that other gods were in fact not real, that there was only one God, and that he had been revealed to the Jews.

Some of the differences between the God of the Jews and the other gods are striking, and they became central to the three major monotheistic faiths. One difference is that unlike the gods of the polytheists, the God who revealed himself in the burning bush could not be named, used, or manipulated. Unlike the gods of the polytheists, the God Moses encountered on Sinai came with no history, other than the rather sketchy record of his encounters with his people. When Moses asks his name at the burning bush, he replies, "I am who I am," which can also be rendered, "I will be what I will be." Moses knew that, in a common ancient understanding, to know another's name is to have power over him. The name of the Lord—that is, the four Hebrew consonants used to render his name, and probably pronounced "Yahweh," a third-person form which may mean "He causes to be"—is never said when it is read by Jews; the word "adonai," meaning "Lord," is substituted. Orthodox Jews writing in English write "G-d" instead of God, emphasizing the fact that this is not a word like other words, or a name like other names.

The God who revealed himself on Sinai is not the God of a particular place or city, as were so many ancient gods; nor is this a God who is remote from human affairs. God is revealed in history and is known through specific events and encounters with Israel, the people God has chosen to make his presence and his will known in the world. God is the one who delivers Israel from captivity in Egypt, who gives Israel the promised land, who allows Israel to be taken into the Babylon captivity, who restores Israel's fortunes. The relationship between the Lord God and Israel is one in which a covenant is tested constantly: the people as a whole may stray, but a remnant remains faithful; the kings may be righteous or wicked, but prophets will be there, chosen by God to tell the king, the people, or whoever needs to be told, where they have gone wrong, why they must repent, and what God demands of them, and sometimes this was done against the prophet's will (see the book of Jonah). Where some gods were strictly local, their power either confined to or strongest in a particular place, this was not true of Israel's God. Somewhere the English theologian and novelist Charles Williams wrote, "God commanded that altars be built, so that he could send his fire down somewhere else."

Although the relationship of Israel to God is unique among ancient religions, it was not unique to the extent of being entirely unlike surrounding religions. Some Egyptian prayers closely resemble the Psalms; there are Job-like narratives in other nearby religious traditions (with quite different conclusions and other morals drawn); and the story of Noah may have entered the canon after the Babylonian captivity. (The Babylonian Epic of Gilgamesh tells the story of Ut-Nepishtam, a Noah-like character, and features a Noah-like flood.) Zoroastrianism also taught that there was a final judgment and spoke of angels and demons. This may have had an influence on Jewish thought, although this is unproven.

What is most interesting about contemporary Judaism and Christianity is that they are more or less the same age. While Judaism as a tradition is clearly older than historical Christianity, the contemporary form of Judaism—based not on temple worship but focused primarily on the synagogue community—is roughly the same age as Christianity. The destruction of the Temple in 70 AD ended one form of Jewish worship; other forms of Judaism present during the life of Jesus—the temple-based observance of the Sadducees and the quasi-monastic Qumran community, for example—died out. The synagogue-based tradition that had its origins in the time of exile from Jerusalem, during the

Babylonian captivity, became central to Judaism and grew in importance even during the time of the Temple's existence because of the dispersion of Jews throughout the world beyond Palestine. The Septuagint translation of the scriptures, from Hebrew to Greek, was meant to meet this need of this diaspora; for many Jews, Greek, and not Hebrew, was the most familiar language.

This parallel history is the reason that some Jewish scholars (for example, the late Samuel Sandmel[2]) have made a point of studying the New Testament. Along with Josephus and a relatively few other sources, the New Testament is a source of information about the years during which synagogue-based Judaism began its life.

It must be emphasized, however, that when we speak of the roughly contemporary histories of Christianity and of Judaism as it is practiced now in the home and the synagogue, we are not speaking of the whole of the Jewish tradition. Jews consider themselves heirs of a four-thousand-year-old tradition that extends back to the patriarchs who preceded Moses—Abraham, Isaac, and Jacob. The feasts Jews now celebrate at home and in the synagogue began to be celebrated long before the birth of the synagogue, and it is in these feasts that we find much of the meaning of Judaism. Although Judaism in its present form is based in the synagogue and the home, what it celebrates includes the Judaism that extends back to the Temple and beyond, into the time of the shrines that are so much a part of the Genesis narrative.

[2]See his *A Jewish Understanding of the New Testament* (New York: Ktav, 1974).

Covenant and Torah

Judaism is based in God's covenant with Abraham:

> When Abram was ninety-nine years old, the LORD appeared to Abram and said to him, "I am El Shaddai. Walk in My ways and be blameless. I will establish my covenant between Me and you, and I will make you exceedingly numerous."

> Abram threw himself on his face; and God spoke to him further, "As for Me, this is My covenant with you: You shall be the father of a multitude of nations. And you shall no longer be called Abram, but your name shall be Abraham [father of a multitude], for I will make you the father of a multitude of nations. I will make you exceedingly fertile, and make nations of you; and kings shall come forth from you. I will maintain My covenant between Me and you, and your offspring to come, as an everlasting covenant throughout the ages, to be God to you and to your offspring to come. I assign the land you sojourn in to you and your offspring to come, all the land of Canaan, as an everlasting holding. I will be their God."

> God further said to Abraham, "As for you, you and your offspring to come throughout the ages shall keep My covenant. Such shall be the covenant between Me and you and your offspring to follow which you shall keep: every male among you shall be circumcised. . . . Thus shall My covenant be marked in your flesh as an everlasting pact."[3]

[3]*Tanakh: A New Translation of the Holy Scriptures According to the Traditional Hebrew Text* (Philadelphia/Jerusalem: Jewish Publication Society, 1985), 23.

This account of the covenant is found in the seventeenth chapter of Genesis, the first of the five books of the Torah. The Torah—the five books of Moses—is what Christians know as the Pentateuch, the first five books of the Hebrew Bible. The Hebrew Bible is usually referred to as *Tanakh*, which is an acronym made up of the three sections of the Hebrew Scriptures: *Torah* (the teaching), *Nevi'im* (the prophets), and *Ketuvim* (the writings). When Torah is referred to colloquially, it can mean the whole of Jewish teaching, including later nonscriptural commentaries.

The Hebrew Bible is at the center of the Jewish religion, but an essential part of the tradition is also occupied by the Babylonian Talmud, which is itself a commentary on the *Mishnah*, a biblical commentary dating back to the second century AD. But these writings are not the beginning and end of Judaism; Jewish beliefs are lived in daily obedience to the *mitzvot*, the commandments of the Law given to Moses (interpreted in different ways, as we will see, by the different schools of Judaism), and the religious calendar.

The Ritual Year

The religious calendar begins with the New Year, *Rosh Ha-Shanah*, in late September or early October. The date varies because the Jewish liturgical year is based on a lunar calendar. The shofar, or ram's horn, is sounded daily as a call to repentance, a reminder of God's sovereignty, and the realization that there will be a divine judgment. Ten days after the advent of the year, *Yom Kippur*, the most solemn day of the year, is observed with a twenty-four hour fast, beginning with sunset and ending at sunset on the following day. No food or drink may be consumed, husbands and wives abstain from sex, and much time is spent in the synagogue. The theme is atonement for sins, and those who have offended others are expected to try to be reconciled to them. These ten days are known as the Days of Awe.

Five days later comes the Feast of Tabernacles, or *Succoth*. For a period of seven days, Jews are commanded to live in booths—temporary shelters meant to remind them of the time when the Israelites wandered in the Sinai desert. Succoth is an ancient fall harvest feast, and the shelters may also recall the shelters farmers erected so that they could complete their harvest labors without having to make the long journey home.

The feast of *Simchat Torah*—the name means "rejoicing in the Torah"—is celebrated at the conclusion of Succoth. The annual cycle of Torah readings begins again, and all of the Torah scrolls are taken from their place in the Ark, where they are usually stored, and carried in procession seven times around the synagogue, while people sing and dance.

Passover is the feast best known to Gentiles, not only because the Last Supper in the synoptic gospels was a Passover seder, but also because many have been invited to celebrate the feast in the homes of Jewish friends. Passover commemorates the deliverance of the Israelites from bondage in Egypt. Each home is cleansed of all leavened products, a reminder that the Jews had to leave Egypt in such haste that there was not time for bread to rise. During the week of Passover, bread, cake, cookies, crackers, beer, and whisky (the latter two involve fermented grain) are not to be consumed.

The seder itself is a meal, observed on the first two Passover evenings, which combines prayer, ritual, joyful song, instruction, a family gathering, and fellowship with invited guests. The text at the center is the Haggadah, which tells the Exodus story, beginning with a question asked by the youngest child present: "Why is this night different from all other nights?" Roast lamb, unleavened bread (matzah), and bitter herbs are eaten in memory of the hasty meal eaten before the exodus from slavery to freedom.

Chanukah is a minor holiday that has assumed what some Jews consider an outsized place as a kind of competitor to Christmas, with an unfortunate attendant commercialism. This eight-day festival commemorates the rededication of the altar of the Temple in Jerusalem. The Temple was recaptured from the Syrian Seleucid dynasty by the Maccabeans. Under Antiochus, the Seleucids tried to assimilate the Jews by proscribing aspects of Jewish practice. The menorah, which is the symbol of the holiday, is based on the story of a single cruse of oil sufficient to illuminate the sanctuary for only one night, but it was miraculously able to provide enough light for eight nights.

Purim is another minor holiday, on which the scroll of the book of Esther is read. Esther was a Jew and was married to the Persian king Ahasuerus. His vizier, Haman, was infuriated because Esther's relative, Mordecai, would not bow down before him. Haman fooled the king into believing that all Jews opposed him and should be exterminated, but Esther revealed his deceit at a party during which much wine was consumed, and the king ordered Haman to be hanged on the gallows he had erected for Mordecai's execution. Purim is a day of rejoicing and feasting, with something of a carnival atmosphere.

The Sabbath is the center of Jewish observance. It is a day of rest, but much more. The family wears its best clothes and has a festal meal; they attend synagogue and engage in religious study, while refraining from labor of any sort. The Sabbath is a commemoration of creation and all of creation's gifts and a remembrance of deliverance from bondage in Egypt. Although attendance at the synagogue is a vital part of the day, the real center of the Sabbath is the home. The day begins on Friday at sundown and ends on Saturday after sundown when stars first appear. (Orthodox Christians will note that this corresponds to the liturgical day in our practice.) Candles are lit just before sundown by the woman of the house, and before the evening meal, the husband pays honor to his wife, and parents bless their children. Blessings are said over bread and wine. The synagogue service on the morning of the Sabbath, during which the reading of the scriptures is central, is the major weekly service. The Sabbath is considered holier than any of the festivals of the liturgical calendar and is seen as a foretaste of life in a redeemed world.

The Afterlife

There is no single Jewish teaching about what happens after death. Jews shared the belief of many ancients that the afterlife would be a shadowy existence (see the story of Saul and the witch of Endor in 1 Sam 28). Perhaps under Zoroastrian influence, and a sense that good people who suffered must at some point receive their reward, the idea that the righteous would be taken to paradise began to become common. The book of Daniel speaks of the resurrection of the dead, and by the time of Jesus' ministry, this had become the subject of debate, with the Sadducees denying the resurrection, and the Pharisees affirming it. *Gehinnom* was seen as a place of punishment for the wicked, but most probably temporary. Most Orthodox Jews believe in an afterlife in this traditional sense, while some liberal traditions emphasize the idea that the deeds of the righteous live on through their influence and good works. In all traditions, the afterlife and what it may or may not be like is seen as less important than what needs to concern us now: a life lived ethically in accordance with what God demands of human beings. In all traditions, there is a place for the *Kaddish*, a prayer of praise to God said in memory of the dead.

The Messiah

The central belief of Judaism is summed up in the *Shema* (Deut 6.4), Judaism's creed: "Hear, O Israel, the Lord is our God, the Lord is one." All idolatry is forbidden. God's people—Israel—have a covenanted relationship with the one God who has revealed himself in his redemptive acts. God's unique relationship with Israel will have its culmination in the messianic age.

The character of what the messianic age, and the idea of the Messiah itself, really means has been the subject of great debate. The arrival of the Messiah means the redemption and healing of the world, the triumph of God's will for the world. Some have seen this in the foundation of the state of Israel and see the beginning of the messianic age in the return of Jews to the boundaries of the Holy Land. Other Jews oppose Zionism of this sort as a form of idolatry.

There are other variations. While supporting the state of Israel, the Lubavitcher movement has been split between those who believe that their deceased Rebbe, Menachem Schneerson, is the Messiah who will rise from the dead, and those who do not believe this, pointing out that before Christianity the idea of a Messiah who will rise from the dead did not exist. Most other Jews consider those Lubavitchers who believe that Schneerson is the Messiah to be terribly misguided; they point to other false messiahs in Jewish history, who were initially met with great fervor and enthusiasm but left their followers in despair when they proved to be false.

Yet most Jews do not see the idea of the Messiah in any of these ways. There are two basic traditions in Judaism with regard to the Messiah. One sees the coming of the Messiah heralded by miracles and marked by a thorough transformation of the world. The other identifies the Messianic order with real political events, such as the restoration of the Jews following the Babylonian captivity by the hand of the Persian king, Cyrus. The medieval Jewish philosopher Maimonides believed that the Messiah would be a king of the house of David, who would bring about a world of peace and justice and gather the scattered children of Israel, helping all of the human race live according to God's will. Many contemporary Jews believe that the idea of Messiah reflects the human desire for the healing and reconciliation of the world, while the more Orthodox await the coming of a specific person, anointed by God (the word Messiah comes from the Hebrew word meaning "anointed"), who will transform the world.

Modern Movements

A post-Enlightenment spirit of toleration led to a growing belief among Jews that Jews could assimilate into European society, allowing them to become part of the wider community. During the early nineteenth century, a reform movement began to spread through European Judaism with the foundation of modern synagogues, which were fiercely opposed by the Orthodox Jews. The emphasis of the reformers was on Judaism as a historical religion, which had known development in the past and which could adapt to changing times. Radical changes were favored by those who insisted that Judaism was primarily a form of ethical monotheism; less radical reformers wanted to preserve traditional observances. The radically reforming wing of the movement—the one that was less inclined or not inclined at all toward traditional observance—was particularly strong in America and Great Britain.

The Nazi era and the Holocaust dealt a deathblow to much of the optimism that had originally inspired the reformers. Reform Judaism today is much more appreciative of theological and ritual traditions. There is, however, still a great deal of tension between Orthodox Judaism and Reform Judaism.

Conservative Judaism came from the more traditional branch of the reform movement and sought to modify Orthodox observance rather than challenge it. Although most Conservative congregations are more traditional than Reform temples, Conservatism's relatively liberal approach to doctrine (compared to the stricter theology of Orthodox Judaism) and some of the ritual changes it has allowed, especially with regard to the place of women, has led to its condemnation by the Orthodox.

Orthodox Judaism itself is divided between the modern Orthodox, who are strictly observant but open to secular education and to a degree of assimilation, and the ultra-Orthodox, many of whom are involved in the Hasidic movement and who stress living separately from the Gentile community and maintaining a radically different, and thoroughly observant, Jewish lifestyle.

The Early Relationship of Christianity to Judaism

All of the first Christians were Jews. But many Gentiles had been attracted to Judaism by a moral code that was more stringent and more ennobling than the pagan standards of the day. From the beginning, there was a strong attraction for Gentiles to a religious tradition that spoke of the human calling and the need for transformation at levels pagan religion did not reach. The earliest Christian writings we have—the letters of Paul—show that from the start Gentiles were drawn to the Christian way; some of them were Gentiles who were first attracted to the synagogue, and others were drawn by what they had heard of Jesus and his life. It was Paul's mission to clarify the place of non-Jews who were drawn into a movement that at first must have seemed to be a mission directed primarily at Jews, as the words of Jesus to the Canaanite mother suggest (Mt 15.21–28). The degree to which Gentile converts should be subjected to the Mosaic laws was the subject of the council of Jerusalem (see Acts 15), when the elders of the Church said that "it seems good to the Holy Spirit and to us" that Gentiles abstain from food sacrificed to idols, consumption of blood (which symbolizes life, and thus is sacred; this is why kosher meats are drained of blood), strangled meats (because blood remains in them) and sexual immorality, but should not otherwise be expected to observe the fullness of the law.

The role of the Messiah was also an issue. At first the idea of the Messiah was associated with King David and the royalty that flowed from his reign. Any anointed king was seen as one who did the work of God in the world and was associated with the idea of Messianic rule. But the Davidic line eventually produced a number of disappointing kings, and after the exile in Babylon, the idea of Messianic rule became a more eschatological one: After the earthly disappointments, the Messiah was seen as one yet to come, someone divinely appointed to bring about the fullness of God's reign, the completion of God's sovereignty, the restoration of the world as it was meant to be. The idea that the Messiah would be divine, or that the Messiah would be a suffering victim, was not a part of the tradition, although the centrality of the Son of Man (see Daniel 7.13–14) and the Suffering Servant of Isaiah may have become conflated with the idea of Messianic deliverance. This was at the time when Pharisaic Judaism and Christianity were making their way into Jewish and proselytized Jewish circles (the Gentiles who had moved first toward Judaism), many of whom became members of the early Christian church.

All these ideas need to be taken into account by Christians, who often write or preach as if the Jews have somehow distorted something that is clearly in the Old Testament, if only they could see it. A Christian who reads about the Suffering Servant in Isaiah cannot help but see Jesus in that role, but to Jews, it may refer to the people of Israel as a whole or to any of the anonymous people who have suffered for God over the ages. In any case, the Suffering Servant and the Messiah were not, to Jews, the same person. The Jewish understanding was that the Messianic age would be a time when God's work would be accomplished. Since the time of Jesus' birth, the world does not seem to be a more reconciled, redeemed, or peaceful place—hence, the need for Christians to posit a second coming. The Christian may acknowledge this, while saying that Jesus is the only Messiah the world is ever going to get, and that the sought-for reconciliation has been accomplished in him: it is the world that has not taken in the message. In any case, the place of the Messiah in the thought of Israel was not clear at the time of Jesus and his first followers, and has been the subject of debate in Jewish circles to this day.

Islam

The word *Islam* describes the attitude of the believer: it means "surrendering" or "submission" to God's will. Muslims—those who are believers in Islam—do not speak of Muhammad as the founder of Islam so much as the last prophet of a truth which went back to Adam, was distorted over the years by Jews and Christians, and was recovered and affirmed in its purity in the Koran, which was delivered in a series of revelations to Muhammad. The Koran (often transliterated Qur'an) is literally God's word from the Islamic point of view. For this reason, it cannot really be translated; to be understood as God intended, it must be read in Arabic, the language in which God delivered the revelation to Muhammad through the agency of the angel Gabriel.

Although Islam is tied to Arabic culture in one central way—the Koran is written in Arabic; therefore, it is a sacred language—it is not primarily an Arabic religion, which sometimes comes as a surprise to Westerners. The country with most Muslims is Indonesia, followed by India. Turks are not Arabs, nor are Iranians, nor are the many Africans who are Muslims. Like Christianity and Buddhism, Islam is a religion that has spread through many parts of the world, adapting itself culturally as it does so.

Muhammad was born around 570 AD in Mecca, and was engaged in the caravan trade. He married a wealthy widow, Khadija, with whom he had three daughters. When he was about forty years old, he felt called to proclaim the worship of Allah, the only God. This was a challenge to his society, which was polytheistic. Allah was one of many gods worshipped in Mecca, the one known as the creator. In insisting that Allah (the word means "God") was the only god and all the others false, Muhammad angered those who profited from the worship of other gods at the Ka'ba, the shrine at Mecca's center. Because Muhammad and his followers were in danger, they found a place of refuge in a settlement some distance from Mecca and, in 622 AD, migrated to the place that later was known as Medina, the City of the Prophet, in what came to be known as the *hijra* (migration). In Medina, Muhammad and his small band of followers rapidly became the most formidable political and military force in the region. In 624 they won a battle over their polytheistic enemies at Badr and, after more bloody confrontations, finally managed to negotiate the peaceful surrender of Mecca in 630. Muhammad died in 632, and Islam as a formal teaching can be said to have been formed during the ten-year period between the *hijra* and his death.

Islam is often called one of the three Abrahamic religions (the other two being Judaism and Christianity)—that is, it traces its origins to the Patriarch Abraham. Christians and Jews are often surprised to see how much of the Jewish and Christian story is incorporated into Islam, and they are also surprised at the ways it is changed in the process. This is because Islam sees itself as the true and uncorrupted faith; both Judaism and Christianity adulterated the true faith by additions or subtractions or distortions over the years. To Muslims, the Koran presents the true faith in its pristine form.

The Koran

The arrangement of the text of the Koran is an ancient convention. After the first *Surah*, or unit—which functions as an opening prayer—it is arranged in units of decreasing length. (The epistles of Paul are arranged similarly in the New Testament.) Muslim scholars agree that the contents go back to Muhammad but not the arrangement. Muhammad himself was barely literate, and written Arabic during his lifetime was more a rough aid to memory than a precise and comprehensive alphabetical and grammatical system. Islamic tradition says that Muhammad received the Koran as a series of revelations, dictated what he had heard, and was probably still at work on arranging the texts at the time of his death. Although the Koran is unquestionably the center of Islamic life, Muslims also revere the *hadiths*, the stories of Muhammad's life and sayings. Much of Islamic law and practice can be found there.

A Christian or Jew who reads a translation of the Koran will find much that is familiar, but with a strange new direction. Muslims believe that Jews and Christians—"people of the Book"—were given God's truth, but that their scriptures have become filled with errors. Their quarrels, both with one another and within their traditions, are adduced as proof of their confusion. The Koran is God's revelation of the truth as originally intended.

"People of the Book! Our apostle has come to reveal to you much of what you have hidden in the Scriptures, and to forgive you much. A light has come to you from Allah and a glorious Book, with which He will guide to the paths of peace those that seek to please Him; He will lead them by His will from darkness to the light; He will guide them to a straight path."[4]

There is an ambivalence in the Koran's references to Jews and Christians. In some verses, they are condemned, and believers are told never to befriend them. They will be punished for their refusal to accept Islam. Jews are seen as having betrayed the Torah, and the doctrine of Jesus' divinity is repeatedly denied. (In one verse Jesus himself explicitly rejects it.) In other verses, Jews and Christians are seen as somewhat confused fellow travelers, and the tone is more benign.

The Koran as a whole is a call for total submission to God and his will, as revealed in the Koran. There is throughout a constant reminder of judgment and of the rewards that await the righteous and the punishment that awaits evildoers and those who fight against Islam. References to characters found in the Old and New Testaments are frequent. Abraham is the patriarch mentioned most often and commended for his absolute opposition to idolatry. Mary and Jesus are elevated, Mary as a model of chastity as well as of obedience. The virgin birth is a firm tenet of Islam. The Koran compares Jesus to Adam: "This revelation, and this wise admonition, We recite to you. Jesus is like Adam in the sight of Allah. He created him of dust and then said to him: 'Be,' and he was."[5]

[4]The Koran, Surah 5; *The Table*, N. J. Dawood trans. (New York: Penguin, 1956).

[5]Ibid., Surah 3, *The Imrans*.

Muslims revere Jesus as one of the prophets and deny that he was crucified. Since prophets are perfect, a true prophet could not meet this ignoble end. (There are, of course, many non-Muslims for whom Jesus' death on the cross is also a scandal and therefore untenable.) It is important to note that when Muslims speak of the prophets they do not mean Isaiah or Ezekiel or Amos; they refer to Moses and the Patriarchs—Abraham, Isaac, and Jacob—and to Jesus, all of whom are seen are Muhammad's forerunners.

Variations of familiar Biblical stories are offered, as well as what might be called non-scriptural *midrash* (the stories told in Jewish tradition that expanded or commented on the scriptures). For example, the idea that Satan's pride led to his condemnation because he refused to pay the appropriate homage to Adam, because Adam was created from dust, is repeated in several *Suwar*.[6]

The Koran also offers a code of living that includes dietary laws, the punishments for specific crimes, as well as the obligations believers have to wives, children, debtors, orphans, and the poor. There is no separation between sacred and secular, that is, between the religious, political, and legal realms, which can also be said of the Bible, for the most part, particularly the Torah. The emphasis is seeing everything in the light of God's will for human beings and their relationship with God and with one another. Although women are clearly seen to have a status inferior to men, in its historical context the Koran was an advance: the rights of women are spelled out, and women are to be treated justly, if not as equal in status to men; polygamy is allowed only if a man is able to

[6]The plural of *Surah* is *Suwar*, which means "chapters."

provide for all of his wives and children; and there are repeated condemnations, some of them quite powerful, of what was at the time the common practice of killing female infants: *Surah* 81, *The Cessation*, speaks of the day of judgment "when the infant girl, buried alive, is asked for what crime she was slain."

Some passages in the Koran will remind Christians and Jews of the Psalms: one praise of God's creation has the repeated refrain, "Which of your Lord's blessings would you deny?"

Islamic Practice

The duties of Muslims are called the "five pillars" of Islam. They include the confession of faith, prayer, alms, fasting, and the pilgrimage to Mecca, which should be made at least once.

* The confession of faith is in a sense Islam's creed: "There is no God but the one God, Allah, and Muhammad is his prophet." This is a rejection of polytheism, of course. But it is also an affirmation of God's complete sovereignty and God's otherness. No creature should be compared with God or be considered as having anything like God's life-giving and life-sustaining power. Muhammad, through whom the Koran was made known, was considered the seal of the prophets, the final revealer of God's word in a line that includes Adam, Abraham, Moses, and Jesus.

* Prayer includes a set of bodily positions, accompanied by the words of prayer, to be performed five times during the day: at daybreak, noon, the middle of the

afternoon, after sunset, and in the early part of the night. Ablutions are done beforehand, prayers are to be said in the direction of Mecca, and although it is best if they are done with other Muslims at the mosque, they may be done privately on any clean ground or on a rug.

* Almsgiving, in Islam, means that a portion of one's annual income is dedicated to charity, to the relief of the poor or to the freeing of slaves and prisoners. This is very much in the spirit of the Koran, which frequently speaks of the importance of charity and says, for example, that a person to whom another owes a debt should give the debtor ample time to repay it; but it is much better simply to forgive the debt.

* The obligation to fast comes during the ninth lunar month, *Ramadan*. This is a commemoration of the time during which the Koran was revealed. From the first light until dark, there is complete fasting from any food or drink. The fast ends with a feast on the first day of the tenth lunar month.

* Every Muslim whose health permits, and who can afford to do so, is expected to make a pilgrimage to Mecca at least once. This pilgrimage—the Hajj—is often described by those who have made it as a powerfully moving experience. A number of rituals are involved, many of them centered on the Ka'Ba, Mecca's central shrine and an object of veneration before Muhammad's time. All of the pilgrims dress

identically, wrapped in a simple white garment—the
ihram—and they often express wonder at the diversity
of Islam. In Mecca (where no non-Muslims are
allowed) they see men and women from all over the
world, of every race and social condition, all equal, all
worshipping together.

One Muslim concept is the subject of much controversy, both
within Islamic society and in the wider world. *Jihad* is frequently
equated with the idea of "holy war," and indeed some Islamic
extremists—often called "Islamists"—do interpret it in just that
way: they argue that Muslims have a duty to expel non-Muslim
invaders by force and have as their goal the restoration of the
Caliphate, the authoritative body which ended with the end of the
Ottoman empire. But many Muslims point to a much more
nuanced use of the word in Muslim history. While jihad can refer
to a war waged for a just religious cause, it can also be seen as any
spiritual struggle, including nonviolent struggles, and as the individual struggle to live a good Muslim life. These Muslims object
to the hijacking of the term by violent extremists, much as some
Christians object to equating "Christian values" with a right-
wing political agenda.

Sunni and Shi'a

After the death of Muhammad in 632, the Islamic community
was ruled by a succession of caliphs, or deputies. They were to
rule Islam as he did but claimed no prophetic role: Muhammad
was the seal of the prophets, the last one. The fourth caliph,
Ali, died in 661. He was a cousin of Muhammad, as well as his

son-in-law. The majority of Muslims—they came to be called the Sunni—believed that the caliphs elected to succeed Muhammad were legitimate rulers; but a minority, later to be called the Shi'a, emphasized the heredity of the prophet. They believed that the caliphate should legitimately flow from Muhammad through Ali, the husband of Muhammad's daughter, Fatima.

The Sunnis emphasized the consensus of religious belief arrived at by religious authorities. But the Shi'a insisted that an Imam in Ali's line of succession would become the spiritual authority for each generation. The twelfth Imam, Muhammad al-Muntazar, disappeared in the ninth century. The majority of Shi'a believe that he will come again at the end of time. In the meantime, the *ulema*, the ayatollahs who have assumed his place, are the religious governors of the community. Shi'a Islam is much more clerical in its emphasis than Sunni Islam.

Sufism

Sufism is an important movement within Islam, which should also be noted. The Sufis stress the soul's unity with God; their mystical movement is quite tolerant of other religious traditions. They are considered heretical by some Muslims but have had a great influence and are an important presence in the former Yugoslavia and Albania (nations close to Europe, which has a cautious and frequently negative feeling about Islam), as well as in many other parts of the Islamic world.

Sufism has aroused opposition from many orthodox Muslims because of its stress on the mystical experience of God's presence, the possibility of sharing in the experience of the divine. The possibility of union with divinity seems, to some Muslims, to compromise God's absolute otherness. But Sufis (much like Orthodox Christians who speak of deification) emphasize the fact that this is all God's great gift, all grace, and has nothing to do with our nature, except our nature as created beings to whom God is merciful and gracious. One Sufi poem reads,

> My God,
> through your direction
> make me dispense with self-direction,
> and through your choosing for me
> make me dispense with my choosing;
> and make me stand in the very centre of
> my extreme need.[7]

In the West, some modern Sufi teachers have downplayed Sufism's Islamic origins, presenting it as an eternal wisdom that resides in all mystical traditions.

The image of a unilaterally intolerant Islam presented by modern Islamists can obscure the fact that, historically, Islam has accommodated a range of interpretations, from the tolerance of Sufism and the relatively harmonious period during the first years of the

---

[7]Ibn Ata'illah, The Book of Wisdom (*Kitab al-Hakim*), Victor Danner, trans. (London: SPCK, 1979), 124, cited by Maureen Clark, "From the Outside In," *Gnosis* (Winter 1994).

Islamic occupation of Iberia during the early Middle Ages, to the puritanical rigor of the Wahabist form of Islam that dominates contemporary Saudi Arabia. When the Jews were expelled from Spain, the majority of them chose to migrate to Islamic countries rather than Christian nations; they could count on more tolerance from Muslims than from Christians. Orthodox Christians used to express the belief that they would suffer less under Ottoman rule, which was Islamic, than they would under Catholic rule, where there would be more pressure to abandon Orthodoxy for Catholicism.

Later Islamic and Post-Islamic Movements

Although the major division in Islam is between the Sunni and Shi'a schools, Shi'a Islam has seen the development of several interesting traditions, which are considered non-Islamic by most Muslims.

The beliefs of the *Alawis* include some elements that diverge from normative Islamic belief in radical ways. Alawis celebrate some Christian feasts as well as Muslim ones; they do not keep the Ramadan fast and worship in private homes rather than mosques. They speak of God in trinitarian terms (though it is not the Christian Trinity), and they have a mass-like ritual involving bread and wine. They believe in reincarnation and have been much influenced by Gnostic and Zoroastrian teachings. The Alawis are essentially a Syrian tribal religion, and though it is a minority faith, its hold is powerful: the ruling Assad family is Alawi.

The *Ahmadiyya movement* is considered heretical because of the place its followers accord its founder. Hadhrat Mirza Ghulam Ahmad (1835–1908) is considered the promised Messiah, the fulfillment of all previous and promised revelations, even the second coming of Christ. Although orthodox Muslims believe that Jesus will return, they believe he will do so as Jesus, not as someone else, so the claims made for Ahmad by the Ahmadiyya movement would seem to supplant Muhammad.

The Baha'i Faith

Although the Baha'i faith has its origins in Islam, its members reject any attempt to describe it as an offshoot of Islam, just as Christians would not want their faith described as an offshoot of Judaism. The beginning of Baha'i history can be traced to a messianic strain of nineteenth-century Shi'a Islam. Mirza Ali Muhammad (1819–1850) called himself the Bab—the Gate—and preached that the promised prophet was coming. Babism faced instant persecution in Iraq and Iran, and in 1848—four years after its founding—Babism declared itself to be independent of Islam. There was a violent state persecution of the Babis and violent resistance on their part. In 1850 the Bab was executed, and after a struggle for succession, a leader in the Baghdad community of Babists, Mirza Husayn 'Ali Baha'Ullah (also spelled Baha' Allah), became the head of what would soon evolve into a new religion. He turned the movement in a more peaceful direction, perhaps under Sufi influence, and preached subservience to the state. In 1863 he declared himself a prophet, a manifestation of divinity. At this point most of the movement had left the region of Iran and Iraq for Turkey; Baha' Ullah himself died in Palestine in 1892.

Within a year or two, Westerners began to show an interest in the new faith, and during the first years of the twentieth century, small groups of Baha'is could be found in Europe and America. A series of struggles for control of the movement led to the establishment of the Universal House of Justice, an institution that brought an end to much of the factionalism that had divided the Baha'is for much of their history. The Baha'i Faith has its headquarters in Haifa, Israel.

Most Baha'is today are converts from other, non-Islamic backgrounds, and the religion's Islamic roots are not part of their understanding of the faith. They see their religion as a strictly monotheistic faith, with Baha' Ullah as the latest in a line of divine messengers, who progressively reveal the will of God to the human race. These messengers include Moses, Krishna, Buddha, Zoroaster, Jesus, and Muhammad, all of whom are in some sense incarnations of God's Word. The early Baha'is were politically passive, a reaction to the violence of the Babist period, but some political involvement is encouraged now, usually of a progressive sort, although obedience to the government is stressed. Baha'is emphasize the unity of humanity, equal rights for men and women, monogamy, the importance of compulsory education, and a just social order. They reject priesthood and monasticism. They are guided by the House of Justice, and their meetings—usually in private homes or rented spaces—and their style of worship is informal. Prayers and devotional texts are read, food and drink shared. There are large temples in the United States, Panama, Australia, Samoa, Germany, India, and Uganda, but these are not ordinarily centers of Baha'i worship; they are used for large public gatherings.

The Islamic origin of the faith has traces in the pattern of religious observance. Prayer is done every day and is done not toward

Mecca, but in the direction of Baha' Ullah's tomb in Acre, Israel. Pilgrimage, usually to Baha'i shrines in Israel, is also stressed. There is an annual period of fasting. Other observances include naming ceremonies for babies, marriage, and funerals.

The Baha'i Faith is still a relatively small religion, with a world-wide membership estimated at four million, but it is making many new converts in India, Africa, Latin America, and among Pacific islanders. The largest concentration of members is still found in Iran, where it has periodically been persecuted. Both its deviation from Islam and its Israeli ties contribute to its difficulties there.

A Note on the Sikhs

This book deals with the relationship of Orthodoxy with other world religions. Sikhism may seem localized, and thus not a "world religion" (it has been estimated that 80 percent of the Sikhs live in the Punjab region of India); yet, there is a growing Sikh diaspora, and the United States and Great Britain have large Sikh populations.

Sikhism is often seen as a hybrid of Islam and Hinduism. This makes some historical sense, just as it would to say that Christianity is a Jewish heresy and Buddhism an unorthodox form of Hinduism, although, of course, neither Christians nor Buddhists would accept those definitions. The Sikhs rightly see their tradition as unique, and although some of their doctrines bear the marks of the shared Hindu and Muslim past, Sikhism itself is a unique form of monotheism.

The founder of the Sikh religion, Guru Nanak, was born in what is now Pakistan in 1469. He was bathing one morning when he had what was a profound and life-transforming mystical experience. After disappearing for three days, he returned home and, after a day of silence, spoke the words that lie at the foundation of the Sikh faith: "There is neither Hindu nor Muslim. Then whose path should I follow? I will follow God's path."

Guru Nanak was succeeded by nine other gurus. Whereas in Hinduism any spiritual guide may be called a guru, in Sikhism the word is used only of God himself, the ten gurus (the last of whom died in 1708), and the Granth Sahib—the sacred scriptures of the Sikh religion. These scriptures are the object of worship and are central to Sikh ritual, venerated by the faithful and read during a ceremony of nonstop reading in the temple; it is also read privately at home. The Guru Granth Sahib consists not only of the writings of six of the ten gurus, expressed in metric verse, but also includes verses from the Hindu and Muslim traditions that are compatible with Sikh teaching.

It must be emphasized that Sikhs believe God to be the only real Guru; the ten who also have the title, as well as the scripture—the Guru Granth Sahib—are called guru because they express God's truth. The ten gurus are not considered to be divine; the word "guru" means a manifestation of God's truth.

Sikhs are baptized through an anointing with and a drinking of a sweetened water. This, as is the case with all-important Sikh rituals, is done in the presence of the Guru Granth Sahib. Although Hindus often consider Sikhs to be heretical Hindus, Sikhism has clearly shed adherence to both its Hindu and

Muslim antecedents. Guru Nanak rejected both the emphasis on asceticism found in Hinduism and the Muslim attention to fasting and food restrictions. The equality of men and women and the unimportance of caste were emphasized from the beginning. Meditation on the name of God is central to Sikh devotional practice.

Although Sikhs are recognized by their turbans, uncut hair (contained in the turbans), beards, ceremonial daggers, and steel wristbands, the true center of the religion is a monotheism expressed in the words of Guru Nanak: "There is One Supreme eternal reality; the true one; immanent in all beings; sustainer of all things; immanent in creation; without fear or enmity; not subject to time; beyond birth and death; self-manifesting; known by the Guru's grace."[8]

A Note on Zoroastrianism

In discussing monotheistic religions, mention must be made of Zoroastrianism. Zoroastrian texts are difficult to date because for much of its history Zoroastrian teaching was handed down orally. Zoroaster began to teach before Iranians had a written language. It would appear, in any event, that Zoroastrianism was the first religion to speak of the resurrection of the dead, final judgment, and an eternal life that is the reward (or punishment) for our life on earth. Some scholars believe that the Jews first encountered these ideas during the time of the Babylonian captivity.

[8]W. Owen Cole's rendering in John R. Hinnels, ed., *The New Penguin Handbook of Living Religions* (London: Penguin, 1997), 336.

Zoroaster lived some six hundred years before Christ. He taught that there was one good and eternal God, Ahura Mazda, who is forced to contend with the Evil Spirit, Angra Mainyu. Our world was created to be the battleground between them. In some of its later formulations, this struggle seemed completely dualistic, as if Ahura Mazda and Angra Mainyu were equals. In the end, however, Ahura Mazda will win, and the dead will be resurrected for a final judgment. The good will be rewarded with eternal life, and the evil will be destroyed in hell. (This teaching was softened in later years to suggest that the evil could be purified in hell and then would ultimately join the righteous.)

We will not go into detail about Zoroastrian teaching; there are relatively few Zoroastrians left. The Parsis in India are Zorastrians, and Iranian Parsis live mainly in the diaspora. They do not seek converts, although this policy is controversial among some members of the community, who fear that without an effort at outreach they will gradually disappear.

What does need to be said is that Zoroastrianism was and is—however dualistic it may have become in some of its manifestations—a profoundly ethical form of monotheism. If, as some scholars suggest, it is the first faith to preach resurrection and judgment, bringing these ideas to Judaism and later to Christianity, there is a profound lesson for us. This may mean that somehow God is at work in traditions outside of Judaism and Christianity and can use traditions outside of our own to teach us something we very much need to hear.

chapter two

ASIAN RELIGION

A sia is the home of a number of religious traditions. The most important are Hinduism and Buddhism, but they have been permeated by influences from other religious and philosophical sources. People formed by monotheistic traditions do well to approach Asian religion with open minds, without expecting to find many features common with monotheism.

There is, for example, no Hindu or Buddhist creed, nothing that has the force of the *Shema* in Judaism, the Creed of Nicaea and Constantinople in Christianity, or the profession of belief in Allah and Muhammad's prophetic status that is demanded of every Muslim. "Dogma" in the sense that the monotheistic religions understand it is not central to being a Hindu or Buddhist. Hinduism and Buddhism are both concerned with the desire to escape the cycle of birth and rebirth: in Hinduism to attain union with divinity, in Buddhism to achieve enlightenment. But there is no one way to reach this goal or one commonly accepted moral or theological path.

Hinduism

Hinduism, the world's third largest religion (after Christianity and Islam), is the religion of the majority of people living in India.

There are significant Hindu populations as well in Nepal, Bangladesh, Indonesia, Pakistan, Sri Lanka, and elsewhere. Taking note of its numbers and its internal diversity, it is difficult to give a simple and consistent description of Hinduism. There are many gods venerated in Hinduism, but many Hindus will tell you that they are really the many aspects of one Divinity. Most religions can point to a founder or originator; Jews can point to Abraham, as can Muslims, who will also say that Muhammad was the final prophet; Christians can look to Jesus, and Buddhists to Siddhartha Gautama, the Buddha whose enlightenment is the origin of all later forms of Buddhism. Hinduism has no such founder, but its roots are ancient.

As varied as its forms may be, Hinduism generally focuses on the belief that the soul goes through many changes, many embodiments (reincarnations), on its way through the universe. All living things have souls, and human beings may be reborn in nonhuman form, while nonhuman lives may be reborn in human form. Karma—the effect of our deeds in one life—will determine what our rebirth will be.

The search for unity with the Divine is at the root of Hindu devotion. Dualism—between matter and spirit, God and creation, God and humanity—is considered an error in many Hindu schools of thought, though others maintain radical divisions between matter and spirit, God and humanity.

Hinduism is an evolving religion and always has been; it is bound more by broad, commonly accepted approaches to ritual and some very general ideas than by any set of doctrines or any dogmatic teaching. Although there is a form of Hindu fundamentalism, often directed against Muslims and Christians, Hinduism has also shown a broad acceptance of all religious traditions, in the belief that they are essentially diverse ways of trying to reach the same goal. The fact that Hinduism has evolved throughout its existence, changing as it encountered new teachings, with minor gods evolving into major ones, is essential to an understanding of a religion that is both ancient and constantly changing.

Hindu Scriptures

The most ancient Hindu scripture is the Rig Veda, a collection of priestly hymns that was probably completed around 900 BC. The Rig Veda is concerned, among other things, with the origins of the universe; not even the gods may know when or how it began. Some of the gods celebrated in these hymns—Vishnu and Shiva, for example— became very important in later Hindu worship. Other Vedas were composed, dealing with cures, victory, success, and sacrificial rituals. Making sure that sacrifices were carried out in exactly the right way was central, and this was the focus of the Brahmanas, which were explanations of the sacrifices. The priestly office gained in power and prestige during the Vedic period, which ended around 500 BC.

During this first period of Hindu history, the idea of reincarnation was not as important as the idea of sustaining the cosmos through appropriate sacrifice. Around the end of the Vedic period, a new set of sacred writings became important. The Upanishads empha-sized the unity of the individual soul (*atman*) with the World-Soul (*brahman*), the basis of the universe, which permeates all things. During this time, the idea that the universe involved endless cycles of birth and rebirth also took hold. This concept of existence as a wheel of suffering—birth, death, and rebirth—which one could escape only with great effort, led to an emphasis on asceticism; the goal was to live lives of such purity that one could break from the cycle of birth and rebirth into a state beyond, called *moksha*, a state of complete clarity and freedom from *samsara*, the condition in which birth and rebirth rule all.

This earliest period of Hinduism also saw the advent of the teaching of the Buddha and of Mahavira, the founder Jainism, an extremely ascetic religion. (Jainism, which teaches that all things have souls and are subject to suffering, taught the important principle of *ahimsa*, or nonviolence—the refusal to cause suffering—that had a great influence beyond its own sectarian boundaries, including the nonviolence that was central to Mahatma Gandhi's message.) Mahavira and the Buddha were heretics, from the point of view of orthodox Hinduism, because they denied the importance of the Vedic sacrifices and the Brahmans, the priestly caste. They proclaimed systems that led individual seekers directly to salvation, and neither was theistic: what mattered was not any god or other form of divinity, but liberation from samsara. But to say "from the point of view of orthodox Hinduism" betrays a Western prejudice, since what later came to be seen as a distinct Hindu point of view was in some ways formed in reaction to the challenges of Buddhism and Jainism, and many Hindus are happy to claim Buddhism and Jainism as part of the tradition.

The Epics

The immense epic the *Mahabharata* and the shorter (but still enormous) *Ramayana* center around wars between human clans, as well as the conflicts of gods and demons (the *Ramayana* involves monkeys and bears in these battles—all of the cosmos, at every level, is involved in the struggle between good and evil, order and chaos). They are, as many ancient epics are, compilations that originated in the oral traditions which recounted a heroic past world, and they took their final form around the fourth century AD. Although they are not considered scriptural in the same sense that the Vedas and the Upanishads are, they are in some ways more powerfully influential. The part of the *Mahabharata* best known to Western readers is the *Bhagavad-Gita*, and among Hindus, it is probably the most popular source of religious inspiration. It is placed toward the end of the epic and reveals an aspect of Hindu theism that will strike a chord with many Christians, even as they see something essentially different in its approach to the idea of incarnate divinity.

The "world-soul" or Brahman is sometimes described as Hindu's creator-god, but this can be misleading. The idea of creation as it is understood in the monotheistic traditions is not found in Hindu cosmology, which knows no single moment of creation. The universe is eternal, going through a series of expansions and contractions; Brahman is the source and sustainer. In the *Mahabharata*, the god Vishnu takes on human form to restore the divine order, or *dharma*, and one of these incarnations is as Krishna. During the course of the *Bhagavad Gita*, Krishna counsels Arjuna, a warrior, on his duty to engage in battle and on the need for action to maintain the *dharma*. One must act, according to one's moral duty—but it is essential that one should not be attached to the fruit of one's actions. Appearing first as Arjuna's charioteer, Krishna instructs him about the relationship of the Atman—the divine within each human being—to Brahman and finally reveals himself in his transcendent glory: "Suppose a thousand suns should rise together into the sky: such is the glory of the Shape of Infinite God."[1]

If Brahman and Vishnu are the gods responsible for the being of the universe and its orderly continuing, a third god, Shiva, is responsible for destruction and radical upheaval. In modern times, these three are sometimes referred to as the "Hindu Trinity" and are seen as three aspects of one God. Brahman, the divine presence that sustains the universe, becomes personal as Brahma, a god who becomes incarnate in Vishnu in order to restore the dharma. But Brahman is ultimately beyond good and evil, beyond what we think of as personality, beyond any qualities.

The idea of dharma is difficult to translate. It means a divine ordering but is manifested in ways that are quite relativistic: some moral codes apply to all, for example, while others change according to one's caste and obligation. The caste system is too complex to explore here in more than a perfunctory form, but transactions between castes are full of purity codes. Purity and the possibility of being polluted are major concerns, particularly to the Brahman castes, the purest. One is born into a caste, caste determines who can marry whom, and ritual obligations change depending on one's caste. Caste can determine what work is permitted, what one may touch (the lower castes do menial funeral tasks, for example), and what foods one may eat. Caste has been used, and continues to be used, in ways that have allowed terrible forms of discrimination. In recent years, however, the idea

[1]Swami Prabhavananda and Christopher Isherwood, trans., *The Song of God/Bhagavad Gita* (Hollywood, CA: Vedanta Press, 1969).

of an "untouchable" caste has been made illegal, with many good results. This is due in large part to the influence of Gandhi. This is not to say that the question of the "Dalit" caste—the untouchables—has been solved; it remains a deep and serious social problem, and many members of this caste, for whom the most menial and degrading work is reserved, have converted to Buddhism and Christianity. But thanks to Gandhi's challenge it is, at least, no longer seen as part of an unchallengeable order, except by Hindu fundamentalists.

Hindu Life and Worship

According to the *Bhagavad Gita*, there are three ways to attain *moksha*, which is liberation from *samsara*, the circle of birth and rebirth. These are *karma* (the way of works), *jnana* (enlightenment), and *bhakti* (devotion). The way of works means that one pursues the ends of one's work ethically, but without being attached to the result or outcome of one's actions. The way of enlightenment (which was the way pursued by the Buddha) seeks a direct and clear perception of reality, and in Hinduism, this is attempted through contemplation and the techniques of yoga. The most theistic tradition in Hinduism is the bhakti path, in which the name of God may be repeated, one tries to be aware of God's presence, and the loving mercy of God is what saves the believer. Those devoted to this path often worship in congregations, chanting hymns and praising God.

Hindu rituals vary with caste, with the Brahmanic caste most invested in their performance. The Brahman is expected to do a sequence of devotions three times a day, rituals that involve purification and offerings. There are also a number of rituals that mark life's transitions: a name-giving ceremony for a newborn child; a ritual tonsure of the child; or an initiation rite in which a young man is given a sacred thread that must be worn at all times. Marriage is perhaps the most important ceremony: it is a duty to past and future generations and involves elaborate rituals, including a procession around a holy fire. The funeral is meant to protect relatives from the impurity that death entails and to allow the deceased to leave peacefully for its next destination so as not to remain as a ghost. Although priests add to the prestige of any particular ritual, they are not necessary to the performance of rituals.

Hindu worship takes place at home and in temples and is, by Christian standards, rather loosely conducted. In the home an area is set aside for worship, usually with a picture of the deity. No one is required to go to the temple, but many people do, and devotion is offered to the image of the god. The statue is bathed, fed, and offered food by temple priests. The number of deities and the treatment of their statues is what has led to the argument that Hinduism is in fact polytheistic, but modern Hindus deny this, linking the veneration of the particular image to the worship of one God who is manifested in many ways.

The Hindu year is full of festivals and fasts; pilgrimage is also important. Where Westerners are tempted to look for clear dogmatic justification for rituals, Hindus rituals are based on the consecration of the year, the times of life, and the stages of one's own passage from birth to death.

Hinduism divides life into four stages. During the first stage, a person grows from childhood to adulthood and becomes educated; the second stage is the householder stage, during which a person marries and has a family; the third stage is the ascetic stage, during which a person gradually becomes detached from material goods, prays, meditates, and studies the scriptures and other sacred writings; and the fourth stage is one of total renunciation— classically it meant leaving all worldly ties to wander as a beggar. This is obviously an ideal pattern—and most people stop at the householder stage—but a significant number of people in India do go the distance and spend their final days as renunciates.

Influence

Hinduism has been influential in the West since the late nineteenth century. In 1893, Vivekananda, a disciple of the important mystic Ramakrishna, went to the World Parliament of Religions in Chicago as a representative of Hinduism. He presented his faith as the world's most ancient religion, the mother of all other religions, and said that all religions were true. His approach to religion was exciting to many Westerners, and he was celebrated on his return to India, where his approach to Hinduism became very influential; it was a major source of Gandhi's own understanding of Hinduism.

Hinduism's open-endedness has had an obvious influence on New Age spirituality, which finds something sympathetic in the idea that we are all heading in the same direction by different paths. Transcendental Meditation and the Krishna Consciousness movement were prominent during the 1960s and 1970s and are still with us in diminished form. A number of gurus have followers in the Americas and Europe. In the guru, a follower finds the idea that the atman can be united to the Brahman fulfilled: by showing devotion to the guru, the follower is brought into contact with the divine. It should be pointed out that the guru does not claim to be divine in the sense that Christians find Jesus to be divine; rather, a Hindu might say that we are all divine by nature, as Jesus was, but must arrive at the fulfillment of that divinity through devotion and ascetic practice.

Finally, it must be said once again that any account of Hinduism is necessarily unsatisfactory. It is home to so many schools of thought that any generalization will invite contradiction. Some Hindu thinkers have rejected notions of reincarnation and the caste system that others insist are essential to Hindu belief; some schools of thought are nontheistic, and others insist that devotion to God is essential. Hinduism is the religion of the majority of the people of India. But its variety and richness have had a worldwide impact, and the ancient religious tradition into which modern Hinduism can be placed is the source of other religious traditions, the most widespread of which is Buddhism.

Buddhism

Although Buddhism's first major field of conquest was in India (there are still Buddhists there, many of them converts from lower castes), its main influence has been felt in Myanmar, Cambodia, Vietnam, Laos, Sri Lanka, Tibet, China, Korea, and Japan. It is a growing presence in America and Europe, with many Western converts from Christian and Jewish backgrounds.

The dates of Buddhism's founding (and the birth of its founder) are unclear. Most scholars agree that the Buddha's teachings can be placed during the fifth century BC, some arguing that the founder was born in the last part of the sixth century, teaching during the first quarter of the fifth century; more recently, the teaching is placed toward the end of the fifth century. In any case, there is agreement that Siddhartha Gautama, born in what is now Nepal, gave up family life to pursue a life of asceticism. The religious atmosphere of the time was one typified by the Upanishads, which emphasized religious knowledge and personal spiritual enlightenment rather than ritual observance. The common story of Siddhartha's life tells us that he was a prince, whose family tried to shield him from the harsh and unpleasant truths of life. He was surrounded by luxury and prevented from seeing any evidence of human suffering or mortality. Despite his family's precautions, on four successive journeys outside of the palace he encountered an old man suffering all the infirmities of age; then a man suffering from dreadful disease; then a corpse. Last of all he saw a wandering ascetic, a sign that there was a way to encounter life without having to filter out the unavoidable suffering attached to being human. (This story made its way into Christianity, in the story of Saints Barlaam and Josaphat, which is probably a retelling of the story of the Buddha.)

Siddhartha left his family and a life of luxury and went to an opposite extreme, starving himself with other ascetic wanderers and beggars, seeking enlightenment. Finally, he came to a middle way, one that avoided extreme asceticism and luxury. Meditating under the sacred Bo tree (Bo is short for *Bodhi,* or "enlightenment"), he attained enlightenment—*Buddha* means "the enlightened one" or "the awakened one."

Much of what we know as Buddhism comes from writings that were not put down until hundreds of years after the Buddha's death. We do know that the Buddhist monastic disciplines go back to the time of the founder: the monks or *bikkhus* (literally "beggars") wandered for eight months of the year, begging for their single daily meal. (This may sound radically ascetic to us, but it was mild compared to the disciplines of other ascetic movements.) But most of the sermons and sayings attributed to the Buddha are the product of later Buddhist teachers. The teachings of the Buddha were originally passed on orally and were not at first committed to writing. Although we have little that can reliably be said to be the words of the Buddha, there is agreement in all of the many schools of Buddhism about his most basic teachings.

First, there are the "Four Noble Truths":

* Existence is suffering.
* Suffering is due to desire.
* Suffering can be overcome only when desire is overcome.
* Desire can be overcome through following the eightfold path.

The eightfold path consists of

* right views
* right resolve
* right speech
* right conduct
* right livelihood
* right effort

* right mindfulness
* right concentration

The eightfold path might look like a statement of the obvious—who isn't in favor of being right in all of these ways?—but their meaning is not entirely self-evident. What does each of these points mean, and how does following this path free us from desire?

Right views means accepting the truth of the four noble truths. Right resolve means taking up the eightfold path single-mindedly, without mixed motives or self-deception. Right speech means avoiding any falsehood or deception, gossip, or idle talk of any sort. Right conduct means avoiding killing—because of this many Buddhists are vegetarians; it also means avoiding all deception and unchastity: monks and unmarried people are to be celibate, and restraint is important within marriage. Intoxicants are forbidden. Right livelihood involves choosing work that is never exploitative, nor does it involve the worker in behavior that violates the rest of the path. Right effort means disciplining the will in such a way that the thoughts and passions that impede progress are constantly struggled against. Right mindfulness means aspiring toward constant self-awareness, shaking off the half-awake, half-unconscious way we usually move through life and, to this end, a number of disciplines help, among them seriously focused meditation, attention to breathing, becoming detached from things that attract us and things that cause aversion. Right concentration is the perfection of this discipline, a steadiness and wholeheartedness brought to the task.

What will be apparent to Westerners from monotheistic backgrounds is the absence of anything like a concern about God. One of the parables attributed to Buddha argues that a concern about such questions—is God real? How did the universe begin?— distracts us from our true dilemma: if you are shot with a poisoned arrow, do you begin by asking for a description of the archer or the size of his bow? Your first concern is to rid yourself of the poison. Our ordinary perceptions and reactions have been so disordered by our imprisonment in the world of illusion that our first and most important task is to wake up. We should remember that the gods to whom devotion was paid at the time of the Buddha's teaching were nothing like the God of monotheism; in Buddhist cosmologies, even the gods were involved in *samsara*, the cycle of birth and rebirth, and the Buddha—the one who was awakened, illuminated, enlightened—was their superior.

The Buddhist teaching that will strike most Westerners as alien is the belief that the self, the ego, is not a subsistent entity. This is a difficult concept: it means that what I think of as myself is not a single reality but a bundle of perceptions tied together in a limited way for a limited time. To see myself as a solid, real, single being is an illusion. This fact is clear to the fully awakened one but can be known only after a struggle. What we see as the self is a composite. Just as a flame seems to be one thing but is in fact a continually burning set of gas molecules confined for a time to one place, the self is a passing phenomenon. There is a continuity to the phenomena we take to be the self, but this does not mean that the self is a subsistent entity, though it may appear to be so.

Before this is dismissed as foreign to our experience of the self, we might ask ourselves what we consider the self to be. Is it the memory I have of myself, growing and changing? A blood clot could cancel that in a minute. Is it my self-awareness? If so, do I, as a self, cease to be myself when I am in a deep sleep or a coma?

Christian mystics have described their experience, in some cases, as one in which the self is seen, next to God, as nothing. This is not quite what Buddhists say. When asked if the Buddha still existed, one early teacher said yes, but that he could not be said to be here or there. How can you point to a flame that has been blown out? While nirvana does not mean annihilation, it does mean that there is no phenomenal personality, no self as we understand it. It cannot finally be put into words or concepts, and much Buddhist teaching is meant to free us from being trapped by concepts.

Theravada and Mahayana Buddhism

Even before Buddhist teachings were committed to writing, the movement had begun to form separate schools. The present broad divisions are labeled as Mahayana and Theravada, but it must be remembered that these terms are much broader than, say, Catholic, Protestant, and Orthodox, or Sunni and Shi'a. The differences between the Mahayana Tibetan Buddhist and Zen Buddhist traditions, for instance, are great. (Indeed, some would say that Tibetan Buddhism forms a third division.) This is in part due to the fact that Buddhism absorbed and included many local traditions on its way across the world. Bon, an indigenous Tibetan religion that includes oracles and shamans, made its way into Tibetan Buddhism; Zen Buddhism, best known as a Japanese form of Buddhism, took its form in China as Ch'an, and was influenced by Taoism. Once in Japan, Zen Buddhism coexisted easily with the native Shinto traditions. Some forms of Buddhism (like the Tibetan) make use of visualization in meditation; other forms avoid it as a potentially misleading distraction. (There is an interesting parallel here with

Christian forms of prayer and meditation—for example, the Ignatian exercises promoted by the Jesuits make use of visualization, while the Orthodox tradition generally discourages this practice.)

Theravada

Theravada Buddhism is found in Southeast Asia, Myanmar, Sri Lanka, Thailand, Cambodia, and Laos. The emphasis is on monastic life, and this has much to do with the fact that it reveres the *arhant*, the person who works individually towards nirvana, an effort that is a full-time work, if it is taken seriously. Like Gautama Buddha, each individual must make his or her own way toward enlightenment. Theravada Buddhists believe they have the original form of Buddhism, "the way of the elders." They have a good case, if what you look at is the earliest Buddhist writing, the Pali canon. But for a couple of hundred years after his first teaching, Buddhism was passed on (as most ancient traditions were) orally, through instruction and memorization. The monastery is central to Theravadan life, and it is an act of piety for laypeople to contribute to the maintenance of monasteries. Theravada Buddhism is, in Western terms, intensely individualistic. The emphasis is on the individual struggle each of us must make to attain wisdom and enlightenment.

Mahayana

Where wisdom and enlightenment are at the heart of Theravada, the Mahayana traditions emphasize compassion. The claim they make is that much of the Buddha's original teaching was passed on orally in ways that by-passed the basic Pali texts, which form the Theravada Buddhist canon, and the many *sutras* that form the sacred texts of Mahayana Buddhism are said to be sermons and teachings of the Buddha himself. Since these texts first appeared hundreds of years after the death of the Buddha, this cannot be literally true; they are, more likely, elaborations of teachings that may indeed go back to the beginning. But the emphasis of the Mahayana teachings is quite different. Monasticism is not so central, though monks are still an important presence. The laity is given a greater role, and there are stories of laypeople who surpass monks in their piety. Compassion becomes essential: not that enlightenment and wisdom are neglected, but compassion is seen as the essential ground of both. In place of the *arhant*, the individual struggler, there is the ideal of the *bodhisattva*, the person who strives to attain enlightenment but remains in the world to help all other sentient beings on their journeys toward nirvana. The bodhisattva could pass into nirvana but remains with the suffering world for the sake of the liberation of all who suffer. There are many bodhisattvas, who precede and will follow Gautama, who had to become a bodhisattva before he could become a Buddha.

Although Buddhism is not a theistic religion, the Mahayana speaks of the "Dharma body" of the Buddha—the Buddha seen as the Absolute. The Dharma body is distinguished from the body of the historical Buddha. This means that the person and life of Siddhartha Gautama are not as important as the Buddha-nature that transcends him; this has been manifested before him and will be manifested again. Many bodhisattvas are appealed to, and there is a devotion to a Buddha who will appear at the end of time, Maitreya. In some forms of Mahayana Buddhism, there is something very like the Christian conception of grace. Pure Land Buddhism worships Amitabha Buddha, who was a bodhisattva in the far distant past and accumulated so much merit that he has an unlimited power to save all who call on his name. He created a paradise for the benefit of all living beings, and those who rely completely on him will attain full enlightenment.

The Mahayana takes many forms, from the relatively ornate forms of Tibetan Buddhism to the spare and intuitive Zen school, which began in China as Ch'an, and spread to Korea and Japan. All schools emphasize the inadequacy of any attempt to speak of Buddha-nature, or the Void. This is at once central to Buddhist teaching and beyond language or concepts. It is the transcendent reality, which can be approached only with a consciousness that is beyond any grasping. Orthodox readers might sense a similarity here to apophatic theology—that is, the understanding that some things are truly beyond language and concept, especially the nature of God. God's energies may be known; God is manifested in God's revelations, in Christ—but God in God's own being is unknowable. In Western theology, the same idea is referred to as "negative theology"—so that when we say that God is good, we do not mean what we ordinarily mean by good, and the same can even be said of God's oneness. God is not one in the sense that I hold one piece of chalk in my hand. In classics of Western mysticism, such as *The Cloud of Unknowing,* this theme is central.

Some Buddhist language has led Western observers to see in Buddhism a life-denying, negative philosophy. After all, the self is extinguished—"nirvana" means "blowing out," like a flame—and the highest reality is Emptiness, or the Void. But Buddhist literature makes it impossible to see this as mere cancellation. What are cancelled are illusion, grasping, and the self-absorbed nature that imprisons every sentient being. What remains is beyond language but is a source of wisdom, compassion, joy, and deliverance to all who begin to approach it.

Much about the Asian religions will seem unfamiliar to Westerners and, in some cases, will not seem to be religious at all. Although there is talk of the divine in Hinduism, there is nothing like the insistence on dogmas and creeds that one finds in the religions of the West. There are forms of Hinduism and Buddhism that seem more like philosophy than religion, and indeed, this is what makes them appealing to many Westerners who are disenchanted with what they have encountered in churches and synagogues. But unlike philosophy, the religions of Asia—while not claiming to be revealed in the same way as the Abrahamic religions—are seen by their followers as mercies, as signs that they have not been abandoned in their quest to overcome suffering and find meaning at the root of existence. The horror of death is not the last word, the universal bottom line. There is more to life than its extinction, and we can experience it—but not as separate beings or egocentric selves. As long as we cling to that sense of self, we are deluded and incapable of understanding or enlightenment.

A Note on Chinese Religion

It is tempting for a writer formed in the religious traditions of the West to distinguish between the various strands of Chinese religious tradition, dealing with Taoism, Confucianism, and Buddhism as if they were completely discrete religions. But, in fact, the practice of many, if not most, Chinese religions involves a use of elements drawn from all of them, and all are seen as part of a common pool of wisdom and tradition. A rough separation, however, can be made. Confucianism deals with morality and ethics, with familial and social obligation, and with the wisdom demanded of rulers and subjects. Taoism addresses our place in the cosmos and nature, and in its appreciation of what cannot be said, its mysticism has much in common with Buddhism and indeed, with the apophatic dimension of Christian mysticism—that is, the understanding that what matters most to us is ultimately beyond the ability of language to express, beyond any conceptualization. Buddhism in China speaks of humanity's ultimate fate, what death's presence and its aftermath mean. But they are all mixed in practice. A Chinese family might celebrate a Confucian coming-of-age ceremony, call in a Taoist priest to bless the beginning of a business venture or to do a healing rite, and a Buddhist priest could be brought in to do a funeral.

Confucius (a Latinized version of Kung-Fu-Tzu) was not acclaimed as a great teacher until after his death, in 479 BC. He was not considered a prophet or in any way divine; he was a wise man, whose wisdom was so deep as to compel the admiration of all succeeding generations. The works gathered around his name are not considered to be sacred scripture and often seem more philosophical than theological, although the heavens are acknowledged, and sacrifice is considered an essential part of a full and good life.

Taoism speaks more of our place in the cosmos and does so in an apophatic way:

> The Tao that can be expressed is not the eternal Tao;
> The name that can be defined is not the unchanging
>   name.
>
> (Tao-Te-Ching)

Chinese Buddhism was the source of many later Buddhist developments, including Zen, which became central in Korean and Japanese Buddhism and the Pure Land school.

At various points, these different traditions were rivals, but they have influenced one another, and in some ways, it makes more sense to refer to Chinese religion as a cultural whole than to act as if these were rigidly separate schools of thought. We touch on Chinese religion briefly because it is not a world religion in the sense that Buddhism and Islam and Christianity are, and it does not seek converts. But, it is the religion of the most populous nation in the world and illustrates one difference between religions in which dogma is important (that is to say, monotheistic religion) and those religions in which it is not. On the one hand, there is a rough division of labor, with Confucianism dealing with morality, Taoism with our place in the scheme of things, Buddhism with death and its meaning for our life. On the other hand, no single strand of the tradition claims that the others are invalid or unimportant, and anyone is free to draw from the whole of this mixed history to celebrate the seasons of life. I venture this opinion tentatively, but in this respect Chinese religion has something in common with the paganism of the Roman empire, where various gods were invoked for various causes, and a deity was sought as a utilitarian aide. Of course, Christians and other monotheists often wrongly use religion this way, but this is not at the core of monotheistic religion. Monotheism makes dogma and the exclusions that dogma will involve central because in the monotheistic traditions truth has been revealed.

It matters deeply, for example, if Jesus was human. We cannot have a serious school of Christianity that says that he was a god dressed in flesh but not really one of us. It matters that he was divine because if he were not both divine and human, we have not truly been taken into his life and with that taken into God's own life. It matters that God is responsible for the whole of creation. Revealed religion cannot admit, as Buddhism can, varying schools where such basic teachings are concerned. We do have offshoots—Unitarianism and such sects as Jehovah's Witnesses, for example—which replicate early Christian heresies. It is remarkable, given the divisions caused by the schism between East and West and the later Reformation, that Roman Catholics, Orthodox, and most mainstream and Evangelical Protestants agree on so much. We see what divides us, but compared to the divisions to be found in the Eastern religions, we are practically a united front. The same can be said of the divisions in Islam and Judaism. Doctrine, dogma, and an agreement on the fundamentals are essential to monotheism in a way that they are not in other religious traditions.

chapter three

ORTHODOXY AND OTHER RELIGIONS IN HISTORY

The First Three Centuries

The earliest Christians did not think of Christianity as a religion opposed to or separate from Judaism. It was Judaism as it was meant to be, a fulfilled Judaism, with Jesus as the revelation of the Father's will for Israel and, through Israel, for a world that now included Gentile believers. Any religion apart from the Israel of God and its Messiah was, by definition, pagan and idolatrous. Even among pagans, there was a desire for more than paganism could deliver, as Paul's reference to the altar of the unknown God implies (Acts 17.23). But the original revelation of the "good news" revealed in Jesus, the anointed one, the Messiah sent to Israel, was not intended to be the start of a new religion.

This state of affairs did not last long. As the Church and the synagogue separated, and as Christianity began to include more and more Gentiles, it became clear that there were now, like it or not, two traditions, and although they professed belief in the same God, they were in sharp disagreement about that God. Jews found the idea of the Incarnation blasphemous. Nowhere was it said that the Messiah would be divine, nor was the world as they experienced it the reconciled place messianic prophesy said it would be. They found it hard to believe that Christians were truly monotheistic, and as the doctrine of the Trinity came to be articulated, they felt confirmed in the belief that Christians in fact believed in three gods.

Christians were faced with this charge from the only serious monotheists of the day. Their other earliest opponents were different: they were polytheistic pagans (to whom they had to insist that they were indeed believers in one God and that all other gods were false) and philosophers (who, like the Christians, scorned pagan mythology). The latter could accept the abstract divinity found in Aristotle and Neoplatonism, as well as the morality advocated by the Stoics, but not the personal, demanding, intervening God of the Jews and Christians. The first attempt at something like a dialogue between these differing religious beliefs was not the open-ended dialogue we often admire in contemporary discourse. It was more an effort to explain the Christian position to Jews and to Greeks whose idea of religion had been formed by Greek myths and philosophy. Understandably, both the Old Testament and the works of the Greek philosophers and poets were used in this endeavor.

It was not an easy world in which to preach the radical idea that the Son of Israel's God had taken on the fullness of a human being in Jesus and that in him alone could anyone, Jew or Gentile, find salvation. (For that matter, it is not easy in our day either.) The Jews had already alienated the Roman empire with their insistence that their God was not just another god for the Romans to include in their pantheon—something the Romans routinely did with the gods of conquered peoples, regarding this both as a sign of Roman largesse and a way of co-opting the subject population. The ethics of the Jews were more rigorous than those of the pagan Romans, a fact that attracted some but repelled many more. The Christians were a new and more threatening group, not only illegal but preaching that the veneration of Caesar, which meant sacrifice to pagan gods, was not permissible.

As Christians began to be threatened by the power of Rome, they found it necessary to mount a defense. They wanted to counter the idea that their aim was subversion and the rumors that, for example, they were cannibals—an idea which was no doubt based on a misunderstanding, or deliberate distortion, of the Eucharistic language about eating Christ's flesh and drinking his blood—or libertines, because of the emphasis on love.

It became necessary for Christians to defend Christianity to the non-Christian world. Spreading the message of Christianity was not just a matter of direct evangelization, preaching the risen Christ. It also involved trying to persuade, by means of the method Paul used, without enormous success, in Athens. Christian apologetics was, among other things, an attempt to persuade non-Christians that the word *Christian* did not mean "fanatic" or "subversive." Christians were monotheists, ethical in behavior, and no threat to the established authorities. In early Christian writings, we find, in effect, some of the first Christian "interfaith" encounters."

In the second or early third century, the author of the *Letter to Diognetus* (his identity has never been established) wrote—perhaps to the Emperor Hadrian, here called Diognetus—to tell him what Christians were really like. The letter begins in what seems to be an ingratiating way, praising Diognetus for his desire to understand Christianity and mocking the beliefs of pagan Greeks and the Jews. It goes on to contrast Christian mores with those that prevail in the empire, including the custom of abandoning unwanted children and casual adultery, and insists that persecuting Christians will only increase their numbers. Finally, it insists on the divine origin of Christianity. While the author attempts rational persuasion, there is obviously no intention here of playing down the Christian claims to be uniquely true.

"Christians," writes this ancient author,

> cannot be distinguished from the rest of the human race by country or by language or by customs. They do not live in cities of their own; they do not use a peculiar form of speech; they do not follow an eccentric manner of life. This doctrine of theirs has not been discovered by the ingenuity or deep thought of inquisitive men, nor do they put forward a merely human teaching, as some people do. . . . They live in their own countries, but only as aliens. They have a share in everything as citizens, and endure everything as foreigners. Every foreign land is their fatherland, and yet for them every fatherland is a foreign land. They marry, like everyone else, and they beget their children, but they do not cast out their offspring. They share their board with each other, but not their marriage bed. . . . They love everyone, and by everyone are persecuted. . . . They are dishonored, and in their very dishonor

are glorified. . . . They are defiled, and yet they bless; when they are affronted, they still pay due respect. When they do good, they are punished as evildoers; undergoing punishment, they rejoice because they are brought to life. They are treated by Jews as foreigners and enemies, and are hunted down by the Greeks; and all the time those who hate them find it impossible to justify their enmity.

To put it simply: What the soul is in the body, that Christians are in the world: . . .

[God] sent the designer and maker of the universe himself. . . . He sent him by whom all things have been set in order. . . . He sent him as God; he sent him as man to men. He willed to save men by persuasion, not by compulsion, for compulsion is not God's way of working. . . .

Do you not see that the more of them are punished, the more do others increase? These things do not seem to come from a human power; they are a mighty act of God, they are proofs of his presence.[1]

Saint Justin, martyred around the year 165 AD, was another early apologist. He defended Christianity and was at once uncompromising in his proclamation of the faith, while trying to make it clear that Christians posed no threat to others. He developed what we first find as a passing suggestion in the Acts of the Apostles. Paul, in Athens, had suggested that Christian thought was

[1] C. C. Richardson, ed., *Early Christian Fathers* (New York: Collier, 1970), 216–219.

implicit in some non-Christian writers. Beginning with a reference to the altar set up "to an unknown God," Paul says that God intended all human beings to "seek God, in the hope that they might feel after him and find him. Yet he is not far from each one of us, for 'In him we live and move and have our being'; as even some of your poets have said, 'For we are indeed his offspring'" (Acts 17.22–29).

In Justin's his first apology, he further developed this argument by denouncing the pagan gods as demons and by doing so drew Socrates into the orbit of Christ and the persecuted Christians: Socrates was telling the truth, and truth can only be associated with the *Logos* of God.

> When Socrates tried to bring these matters to light and to rescue mankind from those demons by the critical application of sound reasoning, then those very demons used the agency of man who delighted in wickedness to secure his execution for atheism and impiety, alleging that he was introducing novel supernatural powers. They are active against us on just the same lines. For not only was the truth of those matters established by Socrates among the Greeks by the application of reason (*logos*), but also among the barbarians by the Word (*logos*) himself who took the form and was made man, and received the name of Jesus Christ. Taught by him, we assert that these demons are not only not good, but wicked and unholy demons whose actions are inferior to those of mere men who set their hearts on virtue. . . . Thus we are called atheists. And we admit that in respect of such supposed

gods as those we are atheists: but not in regard to the
most true God. . . .

Justin finds an implicit Christianity among the ancient Greeks
and Jews:

> We are taught that Christ is the First-born of God, and
> we have explained above that he is the Word [*Logos,* or
> *reason*] of whom all mankind have a share, and those
> who lived according to reason are Christians, even
> though they were classed as atheists. For example; among
> Greeks, Socrates, and Heraclitus; among non-Greeks,
> Abraham, Ananias, Azarias, and Misael,[2] and Elias, and
> many others.

After assuring the authorities that Christians offer worship to
God but "in all other things we gladly obey you," Justin defends
true Christian faith and practice against the distortions and lies of
those who opposed Christianity and then writes,

> I prayed and strove with all my might that I might prove
> a Christian: not because Plato's teachings are contrary to
> Christ's, but because they are not in all respects identical
> with them: as is the case with the doctrines of the others,
> the Stoics, the poets, and the prose authors. For each,
> *through his share in the divine generative Logos, spoke
> well, seeing what was akin to it;* while those who contra-
> dict them on the more important matters clearly have not

[2]These are the Septuagint names for Shadrach, Meshach, and Abednego.

obtained the hidden wisdom and the irrefutable knowledge. *Thus, whatever has been spoken aright by any men belongs to us Christians;* for we worship and love, next to God, the Logos which is from the unbegotten and ineffable God; since it was on our behalf that he has been made man, that, becoming partaker of our sufferings, he may also bring us healing. *For all those writers were able, through the seed of the Logos implanted in them, to see reality darkly.* For it is one thing to have the seed of a thing and to imitate it up to one's capacity; far different is the thing itself, shared and imitated in virtue of its own grace.[3]

In Justin's words, we see a different approach from those Christians who have argued that there are no truths at all outside of Christianity. He says that all truth belongs to Christians because God, through the Word, is the source of all truth, and the Word who took on human flesh in Christ is the fullness of all human truth. But those who even unwittingly have participated in this truth are in some sense in communion with it, however imperfectly, and this is because "seeds of the Word (*Logos*)" are found everywhere.

[3]H. Bettenson, ed., *The Early Christian Fathers* (New York: Oxford University Press, 1987), 58–64. Emphasis added.

Another early example of what can be seen as a dialogue between Christians and pagans is found in the sayings of the desert fathers, the first Christian monks. There we read,

> Abba Olympus said this. "One of the pagan priests came down from Scetis one day and came to my cell and slept there. Having reflected on the monks' way of life, he said to me, 'Since you live like this, do you not receive any visits from your God?' I said to him, 'No.' Then the priest said to me, 'Yet when we make a sacrifice to our God, he hides nothing from us, but discloses his mysteries; and you, giving yourself so much hardship, vigils, prayer and asceticism, say that you see nothing? Truly, if you see nothing, then it is because you have impure thoughts in your hearts, which separate you from your God, and for this reason his mysteries are not revealed to you.' So I went to report the priest's words to the old men. They were filled with admiration and said that this was true. For impure thoughts separated God from man."[4]

Notice that in the Letter to Diognetus, the author assumes a certain common ground, a shared reasonableness about what might be seen as a virtuous life and a desirable community. Justin also looks for reasonable agreement, acknowledging that divine truths may be found beyond the boundaries of the Christian faith, while insisting that the fullness of truth is to be found in Christianity. The pagan priest tells the monks of the desert something they

---

[4]"Olympius," in Benedicta Ward, ed. and trans., *The Desert Christian: The Sayings of the Desert Fathers* (New York: Macmillan, 1975), 160.

acknowledge they need to hear. This was done, and can still be done, without a relativistic understanding of truth.

This approach is, however, not the only ancient Christian tradition. Cyprian of Carthage (d. 258) insisted that "outside of the Church there is no salvation." In his treatise *On the Unity of the Church*, where Cyprian makes this claim, it is clear that he means by this the visible church built upon Peter, and even those who die for the Lord but are not in unity with this Church do not free themselves from the stain of schism. "He cannot have God for his Father, who has not the Church for his mother." This was written in reaction to a particular schism in the Church, but Cyprian's belief that outside the Church there is no salvation—in other words, that those who are not members of the visible Church have no part in the truth—has had a profound influence in Orthodoxy and beyond it. The Protestant who says that no one can be saved who has not accepted Christ as a personal savior; the anti-Vatican II Catholic who believes that those who are not Catholics of the strictest (and these days anti-papal) sorts cannot be saved; or the Orthodox who believe that there is no truth to be found anywhere beyond the boundaries of the Orthodox Church are all inheritors of this tradition. Ultimately, this approach is taken by Christians toward other Christians, as well as toward members of non-Christian religions.

From the Fourth Century Through the Rise of Islam

Once Christianity was made a legal religion, the mild and relatively conciliatory approach of the apologists faded. Paganism made a few attempts at a comeback, but following the failure of

Julian the Apostate to restore paganism, the power of the state was firmly behind the Church; this attempt at synthesis led, among other things, to a lack of tolerance for Judaism—there are, for example, unpleasant blasts at the Jews in the writings of St John Chrysostom. This was only the beginning: the history of Christianity, East and West, saw many periods during which Jews were harried, persecuted, and murdered in the name of the Jew who died for the forgiveness of all, the one who asked the Father to forgive the ignorance of those who, thinking that they were doing something good, crucified him.

It can be shown, however, that this is not the only way Orthodoxy approached other religious traditions as time progressed. While there are the types of statements referred to above, there is also the interesting history of Orthodoxy as it found itself living and contending with the Muslim tradition as Islam began its remarkable spread beginning in the seventh century. While Christians faced with Islam believed firmly that the new religion was a regression, heretical at best, the dialogue often assumed that there was enough shared ground to make reasonable discourse between the opposing traditions possible, even if finally they had to remain at odds.

Archbishop Anastasios [Yannoulatos] has been interested in Orthodoxy's relationship with Islam and other non-Christian religions for years and has written several incisive essays on the subject. As the head of the Orthodox Church in Albania, he lives within a country where a majority of the people are from a Muslim background. Prior to his service in Albania, he served in African missions, where Islam and Christianity are also in competition. In his essay "Dialogue with Islam," Archbishop Anastasios traces the contacts between Orthodoxy and Islam from the earliest years.[5] In the eighth century, St John of Damascus considered it a primitive fabrication and referred to it as a Christian heresy, but the archbishop points out that he also used the word heresy to refer, for example, to Greek philosophy. Not surprisingly, the earliest Orthodox writing on the subject consisted of anti-Islamic polemics. The rapid spread of Islam was alarming, and Islam was aggressive in its attack on such central Christian teachings as the Incarnation and the Trinity. In fact, intolerance often originated on the other side. Archbishop Anastasios quotes the Emperor John Cantacuzenos:

> The Muslims prevent any of their own from engaging in dialogue with the Christians, in order, it seems, to keep them from ever learning the truth clearly, through such an exchange of views. The Christians, however, confident that their faith is pure and that the doctrines they hold are right and true, do not in any way hinder their own; on the contrary, every Christian has full permission and authority to converse with anyone who wishes or desires to do so.[6]

According to Archbishop Anastasios, at first the Byzantines saw Islam as a variant and a resurgence of Arianism. Christians responded to Islam's attacks on the divinity of Jesus and the Trinity by casting doubt on Muhammad's status as a prophet, with some seeing him as a servant of the Antichrist. Comparing the Koran with the Bible, they found it full of distortions and saw a regression

[5]This essay is reprinted in Archbishop Anastasios Yannoulatos, *Facing the World* (Crestwood, NY: St Vladimir's Seminary Press, 2003), 103–126.

[6]Ibid., 106–107.

from true biblical teaching, objecting particularly to the idea of "holy war," the Islamic teaching on the family, and slavery.

But Archbishop Anastasios points out that there was enough common conceptual ground to make dialogue possible. Gregory Palamas, he writes, was

> gentle and patient when it came to the reactions of Muslims. His goal was to persuade his interlocutors; he therefore based his arguments on points that the two religions held in common.[7]

Palamas, who died in 1359, argued as earlier Orthodox writers had that Muhammad was not foretold by the prophets, nor did he work miracles. When Muslims argued that Islam's military victories proved its superiority, he wrote, "[Muhammad was involved in] war and the sword and bloodshed and plunder; none of these things is of God, who is first and foremost good."[8]

Another early proponent of Christian-Muslim dialogue was Emperor Manuel II Palaeologos, who engaged in a series of dialogues with educated Muslims, in which he criticized Muslim teaching and was clear about his adherence to Orthodox Christianity. However, he avoided the negative and disparaging language of the earlier Byzantine encounters with Islam.

[7]Ibid., 108.

[8]Ibid., 109.

Under the Turkish Yoke

In 1453 AD, Constantinople fell to the Muslim ruler Mehmet II. By 1517, with the Muslim conquest of Egypt, the whole of the Orthodox world—Russia excepted—was ruled by Muslims. According to Alexander Schmemann, this had a profound effect on the mind of the Church.[9] But the rule of Islam was not simply tyrannical, although tyranny was often part of it. Schmemann writes,

> In defining the nature of the Turkish yoke, one must first emphasize that it was not a persecution of Christianity. When Mohammed [the Sultan Mehmet] entered the city, after three days of pillages, outrages, and revelry after victory, he announced "law, mercy, and order." He was no barbarian; he had been in Constantinople before and knew Greek. . . . In addition, although the Koran taught that Christians were unbelievers, it recognized Christ as a prophet and showed respect for Him. Therefore one of the first acts of Mohammed after victory was an invitation to the Greeks to elect their own patriarch.[10]

And, this was done with a maximum of respect. Steven Runciman points out that Mehmet gave the newly elected patriarch, Gennadius, the robes of his office, his episcopal staff, and a pectoral cross, saying as he did so, "Be Patriarch, with good fortune, and be assured of our friendship, keeping all of the privileges that the

[9]Alexander Schmemann, *The Historical Road of Eastern Orthodoxy* (Crestwood, NY: St Vladimir's Seminary Press, 1977).

[10]Ibid., 271–272.

patriarchs before you enjoyed."[11] Hagia Sophia had been made a mosque, so the consecration of Gennadius took place at the Church of the Holy Apostles, following which he rode in procession around the city on a horse given to him by the sultan.

As much *noblesse oblige* as Mehmet displayed here, the fact that Hagia Sophia, the great symbol of Eastern Christendom, had been made a mosque was a sign that Christianity was a vassal religion, and Christians were second-class citizens in the Ottoman empire. The heads of the non-Muslim religious bodies governed and judged their own people under the *milet* system of the Ottoman empire, but Christians were made to wear distinctive clothing. Among Christians, only the patriarch was allowed to ride a horse; Christians could not serve in the armed forces (though they were forced into the navy); Christian families had to tolerate their young sons being seized, forcibly converted to Islam, and made to serve in the Janissary regiments; any Christian who converted to Islam—even under duress—and then returned to Christianity was killed; and lawsuits between Christians and Muslims were decided according to the Sharia law spelled out in the Koran. Patriarch Gennadius was opposed by many of his subjects because of his use of *oikonomia*, stretching the laws of the Church to make life less unbearable. For example, he allowed the marriage of boys as young as twelve—in order to prevent them from being seized, forcibly converted, and pressed into military service.

Such was the "interfaith" context of Orthodoxy in Asia Minor after 1453. We have hints also of the dialogue that took place within this context. Mehmet asked Gennadius, shortly after his

[11]Steven Runciman, *The Great Church in Captivity* (Cambridge: Cambridge University Press, 1968), 169.

conquest, for a summary of their conversations about Christianity and its meaning. Gennadius departed from the polemical style of earlier Christian commentators when dealing with Islam. According to Archbishop Anastasios,

> Gennadius writes as objectively as possible about the Christian faith, without directly comparing it to the Islamic faith, which—it goes without saying—is continuously on his mind. He elaborates his own religious views systematically but avoids attacking Islam. He attempts to elucidate issues that are known to be theological points of contention between the two religions, such as the Holy Trinity and Christological dogma, using language that is easily accepted and understood by his interlocutors. The image of the flame is employed to illustrate the doctrine of the Holy Trinity more graphically: "We believe that Reason [*logos*] and Spirit [*pneuma*] arise from God's nature as light and heat from a flame."[12]

Fifteen years later, Gennadius had a discussion with two pashas who wanted to discuss the Christian understanding of the divinity of Christ, since they recognized Christ as holy and even understood him as God's Word and Spirit. He made a point of beginning with those aspects of Christianity that were accepted by Muslims, trying to adapt his teaching to the understanding of his hearers. In taking this new approach, Archbishop Anastasios writes, Gennadius was "clearly responding to the pressure of new historical conditions."

[12]Yannoulatos, *Facing the World*, 112.

Our admiration for Gennadius' mildness—compared with the ways in which earlier Orthodox had written of Islam—should be tempered by the understanding that he had little choice. In countries where the situation was reversed, Orthodoxy was not so mild. St Vladimir of Kiev and other Orthodox leaders—like many Christian rulers, Catholic, Orthodox, and later Protestant—had no problem with forced conversions. It became a rule of sorts that the religion of the prince was the religion of his people. The much later Enlightenment idea of religious tolerance was an outgrowth of the failure of this arrangement. The secularism of the Enlightenment, with its insistence on religious toleration, was in large part a result of Europe's exhaustion following the religious conflicts of The Thirty Years' War (1618–48). The separation of church and state embodied in the American legal tradition is a direct outgrowth of this.

A look at the history of religion makes it clear that where a religion rules over religious minorities, the most that can be hoped for is the sort of *noblesse oblige* shown by Mehmet to Gennadius; the worst that can happen shows up in inquisitions and pogroms. Tolerance was not, in general, a religious tradition.

The relatively temperate and diplomatic approach of Patriarch Gennadius, Emperor Manuel II Palaeologos, and the early apologists have something to tell us today. The history of religion in power is the best argument for the Enlightenment's desire to weaken its institutional clout. There is a certain wisdom, not of secularism, but of something that secularism has taught us: if religion is to be a vital part of the culture, it must *persuade*. It is not a bad thing for the Church to be limited to persuasion, and it is probably no coincidence that in those countries where churches are established and propped up by the state, they are generally unpersuasive to the majority of the population, who show their lack of interest by nonattendance. The relative health of religion in America, as compared to the subsidized churches of many European nations, where almost no one attends church, might be a good argument for the separation of church and state.

Another interesting phenomenon can be observed in those situations where Orthodox and other Christians are in a religious minority. In South India, Lebanon, and Syria, Orthodox and other Christians cooperate more easily with one another than they do in lands where one or another Christian religion enjoys a powerful position, and their relationship with the non-Christian majority tends to be a relatively relaxed one. Orthodox and Melkite Catholic Christians have a more cordial relationship in Syria and Lebanon, for example, than Orthodox and Eastern-rite Catholics do in regions where Orthodox or Catholics predominate. This can be seen cynically: when you have power you behave like a tyrant; when you do not, you become conciliatory. Christians have never claimed to be exempt from human failing—after all, we are the ones who talk about the Fall and Original Sin—but something more is going on here. Where Christians are all members of a minority, they are more inclined to see and celebrate what unites them than to argue bitterly about those sometimes relatively few points that divide them, and this becomes more apparent when they are surrounded by a non-Christian majority population. Being a member of a minority religion means that you must explain, to yourself, your children, and your neighbors, exactly why you believe what you believe. As with the first Christians, one way of doing this is seeking a point of common understanding, a shared vocabulary.

Our situation today can be seen as not all that different from the world the early apologists had to address. Orthodoxy must now make itself known and understood in a world where no religion has a privileged place. Some may mourn this fact, but it may be a new and profoundly important opportunity.

chapter four

HOW OTHER CHRISTIANS
APPROACH THE DIALOGUE

I n trying to arrive at an Orthodox Christian view of non-Christian religions and our relationship to those who believe in them, it is important to consider the ways other Christians approach the matter. When we do this, we find responses that range from total rejection of any dialogue to a complete acceptance of the idea that other religions are as valid in their ways of seeking and finding divine truth as Christianity is. A consistent pattern proves elusive. The following brief summary is hardly exhaustive, but it may serve to open a window onto the current state of the discussion about the relationship of Christianity to non-Christian religions.

Fundamentalists, and many evangelicals, take a position that may be described as *Total Replacement*—that is, Christianity necessarily replaces all other forms of religious understanding, which are false.[1] Karl Barth, probably the greatest Protestant theologian of the twentieth century, acknowledged that many good

---

[1] I owe a debt, throughout this chapter, to Paul F. Knitter's *Introducing Theologies of Religion* (Maryknoll, NY: Orbis Books, 2003). Knitter's categories are extremely helpful generalizations, and I borrow them shamelessly.

and beautiful elements may be found in non-Christian religions, but Christian revelation shows "religion" to be "a human attempt to anticipate what God in His revelation wills to do and does do. It is the attempted replacement of a divine work by a human manufacture."[2] Barth felt that this could also be true of Christian religion, whenever we rely on anything other than faith, grace, and Christ.

Other evangelicals have proposed another model, one of *Partial Replacement*. They point out that Paul speaks of the law's requirements as written on the hearts of Gentiles, with their conscience bearing witness (Rom 1.20, 2.15), and Paul's words to the Athenians in Acts 17 imply that God has worked outside the boundaries of Judaeo-Christian revelation. Knitter quotes John Calvin, who said that a natural human "sense of God" meant that "the knowledge of God and of oneself is connected by a mutual bond."

So God can be seen to have been at work in other religions. It is, however, necessary to insist that it is the God of Israel who saves through Jesus Christ, and without Christ, there is no salvation. God may make use of other religions to move people toward himself, but Christ is the only savior. While evangelicals are divided as to whether those who do not explicitly accept Christ before their deaths can be saved—some believe God may offer a choice after death—if anyone is saved, a decision for Christ is essential.

A different model, the one most common in Roman Catholic and mainstream Protestant thinking and shared by many Orthodox, is that of *Fulfillment*. Perhaps the greatest proponent of this point

[2]Knitter, *Introducing Theologies*, 25.

of view was the Catholic theologian Karl Rahner. From this perspective, God can and does work through other religions to save people. At the same time, all grace comes through Jesus Christ. Those who belong to other religions may experience God's love and grace and may be saved by taking it to heart within the context of their own religion, but even though they may not be aware of it, what saves them is the grace of God, which has been fully revealed only in Jesus Christ. They are, in Rahner's (questionable) formulation, "anonymous Christians."

With the *Mutuality* model, we enter new and stranger territory from the point of view of traditional Christianity. This approach to other religions moves away from the "exclusivist" vision of the other models, which means that Christianity is not the only true faith, and Christ is not the only way to salvation. Knitter prefers the phrase "mutuality" to an alternative that is often offered, "pluralist," because it emphasizes the relationships between the religions, that is, the dialogue. Pluralism might imply simple tolerance rather than a conversation in which the dialogue partners might really learn from one another. Without denying the real differences between religions (by saying something like "we are all really saying the same thing"), this model privileges no particular religion. No one religion may claim to be the final or only way of salvation or source of saving grace. To say that any one figure, teacher, or savior is the way for all the others—whether this must be acknowledged in this life or arrived at in eternity—is to eliminate serious dialogue, in which each party is taken with equal seriousness.

The philosopher John Hick has recommended that we move from a Christian, or Jesus-centered, model to a God-centered model, but even this must be modified, since Buddhists are not theists. In doing so a kind of ultimate reality or divine reality becomes something that religions point toward without encompassing it. All the great religious traditions distinguish between a divine reality that is ultimately beyond any human understanding and the various ways in which human beings have experienced this reality and express it. In all traditions, there is at the center something more than can be articulated, something beyond words or concepts. This "more," this inexpressible reality, is what is emphasized in this model. At the same time, those who are considered saintly or holy in any of the religions have much in common, whatever tradition they may come from. This is an indication that the religions may have a common grounding and all are based in something real.

Many contemporary theologians who are involved in the study of other religions take what is called a Spirit-based approach, rather than one based in traditional Christology. The Spirit is more diverse and capable of more manifestations than the Logos. The Spirit "blows where it will," they argue, and thus can be manifested in places other than Christianity. There is a frequent appeal to mystical experience, and a belief that while Jesus speaks clearly to the Christian soul, this does not mean that the experience of the Hindu or Buddhist is in any way lacking. What we perceive as the spirit of Christ may be manifested elsewhere in other forms.

Another way of approaching Jesus, from this point of view, is as a sign or sacrament, a revealing of God. This does not mean that Jesus is unique in this way. The Catholic theologian Roger Haight, a defender of the idea of Spirit Christology, has written that since Jewish and Christian scriptures have recognized that God has worked throughout the world, a Spirit Christology "is open to other mediations of God. The Spirit is spread abroad, and it is not necessary to think that God as Spirit can be incarnated only once in history."[3]

Finally, there is the *Acceptance* model, which does not seek to find the common ground in all religions, as that would blur important differences. This is in some ways a "postmodern" model, in that it does not assume, as much post-Enlightenment thought does, the power of reason to unpack reality and find truth in a direct way, since there will be a variety of ways to read a particular tradition or set of traditions. The fullness of God's mystery and presence cannot be captured in any human language or set of symbols; furthermore (and here the strong influence of modern philosophy is found), we should not be too seduced by the Enlightenment's faith in the power of individual rationality to discern the world clearly. We are born into languages and symbol-systems, including religious ones, which to a large extent form our experiences of religion and guide our religious understanding. Knitter cites George Lindbeck, arguing against the idea that all religions express the same themes in different ways: "Adherents of different religions do not diversely thematize the same experience, *rather they have different experiences*. Buddhist compassion, Christian love, and . . . French Revolutionary *fraternité* are not diverse modifications of a single fundamental human awareness, emotion, attitude, or sentiment, but are radically (i.e., from the root) distinct ways of experiencing and being oriented toward self, neighbor, and cosmos."[4]

---

[3]Roger Haight, *Jesus, the Symbol of God* (Maryknoll, NY: Orbis, 1999), 456.

[4]George Lindbeck, *The Nature of Doctrine: Religion and Theology in a Postliberal Age* (Philadelphia, PA: Westminster Press, 1984).

This model does not allow for easy dialogue but suggests that from within each tradition people will have to find their own reasons for wanting to have a dialogue. Paul Griffiths, a Catholic theologian, argues that every honest religious believer truly believes that his or her religion is the best and the others to some extent are lacking. Griffiths sees the need for the re-introduction of apologetics, in which believers will be able to argue frankly that believers in other traditions are wrong.[5] This can be done with compassion and with an openness that can learn from the other, but this learning will deepen and enhance the quality of the dialogue without watering down or distorting the real differences that exist.

There are Orthodox who will identify with a few of these approaches. We certainly have our advocates for something like the Total Replacement model. Those that take this approach apply it, in fact, even to other Christian denominations: outside of Orthodoxy no truth may be found. But this is an extreme approach, and most Orthodox will be sympathetic to the Fulfillment model—the idea that there is truth to be found in other religious traditions, and God may save non-Christians who are faithful to their traditions. (But, if they are saved, it will be through Christ.) Some aspects of the postmodern Acceptance model are also appealing. We cannot prove or disprove, in some scientific way, the truth of our own belief. But Paul Griffiths's argument for a renewed apologetics is important. Christians cannot, for example, surrender their belief in the Incarnation, however much it may bother Muslims and Jews. Their arguments must take the other view seriously and

[5] Paul Griffiths, *An Apology for Apologetics* (Maryknoll, NY: Orbis Books, 1991).

must see the other compassionately, but they may not, for reasons of a misplaced sense of courtesy, water down the central beliefs of the Christian tradition.

The Mutuality model presents serious problems for orthodox Christianity—by which I mean not only Eastern Orthodoxy, but the tradition of Christianity broadly held by Orthodox, Catholics, and Protestants until the twentieth century. The problem with a "Spirit Christology" lies with its potential to move us from what has been the basis of orthodox Christian belief: in Jesus Christ we learn, as we could not before he came to share our life, what kind of God the Father is, and who the Holy Spirit is. The orthodox Christian understanding is put powerfully in the anaphora of the Divine Liturgy of St Basil the Great:

O Master, Lord, God, Father almighty . . . you are the Father of our Lord Jesus Christ—the great God and Savior, our hope, who is the image of your goodness, the seal of your true likeness, showing forth in himself you, O Father. He is the living word, the true God, the eternal wisdom, the life, the sanctification, the power, the true light. Through him the Holy Spirit was revealed—the spirit of truth, the gift of sonship, the pledge of future inheritance, the first fruits of eternal blessings, the life-creating power, the fountain of sanctification, through whom every creature of reason and understanding worships you and always sings to you a hymn of glory, for all things are your servants.

Among those "all things" may be the holiest aspects of other religious traditions, but the truth toward which they lead their

followers will be the truth shown forth at Pascha—the holy pas-
sion and resurrection of Jesus Christ.

chapter five

ORTHODOXY AND OTHER RELIGIONS IN TODAY'S WORLD

Orthodox Christians frequently—and accurately—point out that the Orthodox Church is the apostolic church. But just as the beginning of the Church at Pentecost as an historical moment marks its antiquity, Pentecost as a present reality is its present vocation. As Orthodox Christians, we are called to witness to the presence of the Holy Spirit in the Church, the Spirit who leads us to show in our lives that Christ is in our midst. Since the movement of Orthodox Christians to countries outside of Orthodoxy's traditional orbit of influence, and since the fall of the Soviet Union and the movement of many Russian Orthodox intellectuals into European and American society, the Orthodox Church has known an intellectual renaissance and a new self-consciousness as it tries to explain itself to Christians whose understanding of the Church was formed by a very different history. In Russia, Greece, and Romania, Orthodox thinkers began to engage modernity in exciting ways, and in Western Europe—especially during the period between the world wars in the twentieth century—an impressive theological renewal took place. In all of the Christian churches, there was a move toward the sources, something that led Catholic and Protestant theologians to their own renewed interest in the Fathers and the history of the liturgy. Russian émigré theologians in Paris were very much a part of this renewal. Alexander Schmemann, Sergius Bulgakov, Nicholas Afanasiev, Georges Florovsky, and John Meyendorff—all associated with St Sergius Institute—did important work in theology, church history, and liturgical studies. In Greece, a similar renaissance took place. Florovsky, Schmemann, and Meyendorff came to the United States, and through them and other European émigrés, the fruits of this theological renewal found its way at first into American Orthodox seminaries and gradually into American Orthodox parishes. Parish priests in the United States were, in the early years of the American Orthodox experience, trained by bishops and other pastors in a rather haphazard fashion; now a seminary education is the norm, and a typical priest will be acquainted with the works of Metropolitan John Zizioulas, Fr John Meyendorff, Fr Alexander Schmemann, Fr Dimitru Staniloae, Fr Georges Florovsky, and Bishop Kallistos Ware, among many others.

Orthodoxy has also had to learn how to live in parts of the world where many or most people are not Christian, either because they are members of another religion or because they are hostile or indifferent to any religious belief. It must make its beliefs clear in this new situation, and this will involve listening to others who come from very different understandings of Christianity and of the relationship between the Church and the surrounding society. Just as Russian Christians during the eighteenth century encountered the non-Christian aboriginal people of Alaska, in more recent years Orthodoxy has moved into sub-Saharan Africa, Indonesia, the Philippines, and Japan; it has had to contend with what amounts to the re-evangelization of countries in which Orthodox Christianity was severely circumscribed or, as in the case of Albania, nearly completely eliminated. In some ways the most ancient of Christian churches is one of the youngest, where its self-understanding is concerned, because of these new situations.

Because of all this movement, the Church is where it was at its beginning. Once again, we need people like the apologists—people who can make the Christian message known in ways that make sense to people where we meet them. In many ways, our task is more difficult than it was for the first Christians, who preached something truly new to the world. Now we try to bring the Christian message to a world that has known Christianity, with its saints, its holiness, and its moral victories—and its pogroms and inquisitions, its crusades and prejudices, its violent conquests in the name of God. How do we present Christianity as good news, despite so much that is negative in Christian history? A beginning might be made by focusing on the work of those institutions (hospitals, orphanages, kitchens set up to feed the poor) that incarnate the spirit of the Church at its best and have done so from the Church's earliest years. Much that secular people now take for granted as part of a shared moral understanding was given to the world by Christianity. Another important focus is the saints. The Russian Orthodox Church at the time of the life of St Seraphim of Sarov was far from a healthy, exemplary Christian community, but he was able to live the truth of the gospel in a way that illuminates us today. The Catholic Church was equally corrupt when St Francis of Assisi was moved to give his life completely to Christ.

This sense of the Church is what we must bring to the dialogue—the Church that came to fruition in the lives and works of its holiest people and that is honest about its failures to live up to its own preaching.

A word must be said about "dialogue" in our contemporary sense of the word: as the quotations from the earliest encounters with Islam make clear, whether the tone was polemical or conciliatory, the Christian side of the dialogue conceded nothing, and there was no moving away from the belief that Christianity was true. Until quite recently this was the norm. In recent years, the meaning of "dialogue" has shifted. Our contemporary use of the word means not only a conversation between two people, equally convinced of the truth of their respective positions; the assumption is that something may be learned from the encounter. While one religion may indeed learn something from another, there are forms of dialogue that show a willingness to surrender points that are essential—the idea that some truths matter more than others and that while we may learn from the other, we must not betray what we have been given by implying that religious truth can be taken in a totally subjective way. There is a sense among many Christians that the dogmatic essence of Christianity is a personal preference, a matter of taste, and not something grounded in the will of God for the whole of creation. Put baldly, there are some people who are willing to say, "Jesus is the way I understand my relationship to God and salvation, but your way may be different, and just as true for you as Jesus is for me."

This is not so much tolerant and open-ended as it is fuzzy thinking. It is all right for me to say that my love of jazz and your love for opera may be different but equally legitimate. It is another to look at what, throughout history, orthodox Christianity has actually claimed, and then to say, "but Jesus may not really have saved you, though I will say he saved me." That describes, at best, a vague sort of mood, not a belief or even something logically defensible. This sense of religion as a private taste, something totally interior and subjective, concedes too much to the spirit of the age and its secular assumptions.

Just as Christians of the first centuries had to become conversant with the philosophical presumptions of their interlocutors, Orthodox Christians and other religious thinkers need to understand the presuppositions of those whose assumptions are based in materialism and an agnostic or atheistic point of view. There is an interesting paradox here: the Christian will find that he or she finds it easier to talk with a Buddhist, Muslim, Hindu, or Jew than with a firm believer in secularism, someone who adheres to what might be called the religion of scientism. Writers such as Richard Dawkins and Steven Pinker—both Darwinist materialists, for whom a materialistic and atheistic accounting of everything human is sufficient—assume they know what believers mean when they speak of God or a spiritual realm, but then present pictures of religion that only the crudest fundamentalist would agree with. To them, however, it is all the same, and there is no need to investigate a phenomenon they scorn without beginning to understand it or to make a serious effort to see how people might disagree with their reductive view of reality. But this thorough-going materialism too must be understood because it is a pervasive phenomenon; we could even call it an unacknowledged religious faith, especially among academics.

Once I heard the philosopher A. J. Ayer lecture at the University of Notre Dame. He denounced the idea of God or "the One," as some Hindus and Neoplatonists would have it because no object could be found in the universe to correspond with such language, which was, therefore, meaningless. One graduate student (a Hindu student of mathematics—he later went into philosophy) stood up during the question and answer period and said, "There are some people who call the idea of God or the One meaningless. There are also people who find no meaning in music. We call these people tone-deaf."

It was a wonderful response and an accurate one, but we need more than that. Orthodox scholars and theologians must learn the vocabulary that has informed modern philosophy, not all of which tends toward atheism. It is not enough to offer updated retreads of the patristic classics; one has to engage the language of one's own context, including the scientific and the philosophical. The philosophical approaches of Husserl and Wittgenstein, very different thinkers, offer fascinating ways to discuss the whole idea of embodiment—something that should be of interest to those who must try to discuss the idea of the Incarnation.

The most educated people the earliest Christian thinkers had to persuade were not believers in the pagan pantheon; one reason the early Christians referred so respectfully to Plato and Socrates was that Plato disdained the idea of the pagan gods and was, for this reason, considered an atheist—as were the early Christians, who were saying to those Greeks and Romans who could be persuaded to accept the relatively deistic position of Aristotle and Plato, "We are more like you than you think, and also very different." But to be able to speak this way, they needed to know Aristotle and Plato. It is important for Christians involved in discourse with secularists not to be philosophical or scientific illiterates. We are, after all, dealing with people who think that all Christians believe that the universe came into being in six twenty-four-hour days. They should not be able to dismiss us that easily. But sometimes the best arguments of their Christian opponents do not get much more interesting than arguments from the complexity of nature (the watch found on the beach implies a watchmaker, and the complexity of, for example, the human eye implies an intelligent designer). There are more compelling lines of argument, one of which is that there is really no conflict between Christian faith and science, unless the Christians argue along strictly fundamentalist lines that the Biblical account of creation is true *as science*. But a similar fundamentalism is at work with materialists who believe that Christians think of the soul as a kind of ghost that inhabits us and that every important human fact can be adequately accounted for by the scientific method, which, after all, is limited to those things that can be weighed, measured, and duplicated and falsified in an experimental way. Can this really be said of love, loyalty, our tendency to be drawn toward beauty and self-sacrifice—none of which make sense at a completely materialistic level?

The topic of this book is our relationship with non-Christian religions, but I mention this form of materialistic secularism because it really is religious, in that it relies upon some axioms that are neither provable nor refutable and requires that you believe them to be true. This includes the belief that only those things that are scientifically demonstrable (meaning that they can be measured and replicated or provable as true or false) are meaningful and that everything else falls into the realm of the subjective.

As far as other religions are concerned—the ones that recognize themselves as religions—the dialogue will change depending upon what we have in common with them and where we differ. What follows is by no means an exhaustive list of suggestions, but it may indicate the way inter-religious dialogue can proceed and, indeed, is going on in some circles. I will take up the different religious traditions in the order they appeared in the first chapters of this book. What I offer here is not a list of the ways in which we can persuade Buddhists, for example, that they are wrong and we are right. Rather, I want to suggest what the encounter might teach us, which will lead us to see both what makes Christianity's claims unique, in the light of our encounter, and the depths of our differences, many of which cannot and should not be overcome by dialogue.

We must bear in mind that in encountering another religious tradition we encounter something that is in at least some degree truth bearing. Archbishop Anastasios writes,

> Everything on earth lies within the sphere of influence of God, the spiritual Sun of Righteousness. One could see the various aspects of religions as "accumulators" charged with the rays of divine truth from the Sun of Righteousness, with an experience of life and different lofty concepts and grand inspirations. Such accumulators have aided humanity by giving the world an imperfect light, or

a few reflections of light. But they cannot be regarded as self-reliant, and lack the capacity to take the place of the Sun itself.

The criterion for Orthodox remains the Son and Word of God, who embodies the love of God in Trinity within history, as it is experienced in the mystery of the Church. Love, as revealed in his person and his work, constitutes for the Orthodox believer the essence and at the same time the acme and fullness of religious experience.[1]

Judaism

The relationship between Christianity and Judaism is in some ways more prickly than the relationship between Christianity and any other non-Christian religion. In part this is because of the filial relationship between the two. The meaning of Christianity cannot be considered apart from the meaning of the "Israel of God" (see Galatians 6.16), and the God in question is Abraham's God, the God who delivered his people from Egypt and gave Moses the tablets of the Law. When Paul refers to the Scriptures, he is not referring to the New Testament (which at the time of his writing did not exist) but to the Hebrew Scriptures and their Septuagint translation, with its additions. Even without the terrible history of Christian anti-Semitism, this would be a difficult encounter, and what makes it most difficult are the claims of Christianity that God has sent his promised Messiah in the form of Jesus Christ and—more shocking still—that the fully

---

[1] "Orthodox Relations with Other Religions," Elizabeth Theokritoff, trans., *Sourozh* (Nov. 2001): 16.

human Jesus Christ is also truly divine, sharing the nature of the Father completely.

This central aspect of Christianity strikes Jews as blasphemy. True, many ecumenically inclined Jews speak politely of the fact that Christianity allowed many non-Jews to accept the Hebrew Bible as something that would help them shape their lives and their sense of morality, and they admire many Christian figures. Yet the central Christian claim—that the unknowable God who created the universe from nothing, the God who spoke to Job from the whirlwind, the God upon whom Moses could not look and live, became a human being who had limited knowledge, who grew thirsty, who agonized and wept over the death of a friend, who even died a shameful death on the cross, a death reserved for small-time rebels and petty thieves—appears to be a diminution of God's being, a form of sacrilege, even idolatry.

They, however, are not wrong for perceiving this in such extreme terms because if we Christians are wrong about this, we are indeed blasphemous. We Christians would be disturbed by the claim of anyone other than Jesus to be divine; we reject Reverend Moon's hints that he is the Messiah even without examining them deeply, even as we would reject the leadership of Jim Jones or any other false prophet. Christians have sometimes acted as if the center of Jewish belief is that Jesus was not God, as if the religion of the Jews was formed by what Christians have seen as a rejection of an offer. We would find it preposterous if a member of the Unification Church said that Christianity is based on a rejection of the belief in the messianic role of Sun Myung Moon, but it is just this type of argument that the Jews have encountered in some of what has passed for dialogue with Christians.

As we approach any encounter with Judaism, we must bear two things in mind. The claim that the Messiah would be divine is not found in the Old Testament. The Messiah, when he came, would lead all humanity into a place of peace and reconciliation. We may say that the Messiah's divinity is a revelation that comes with Jesus' resurrection and ascension, and the sending of the Holy Spirit, and we may have to speak of a second coming in which the fullness of messianic prophecy will be realized at last. But we will not get anywhere by proof texting from Scriptures that Jews understand quite differently. For example, the Suffering Servant in Isaiah 53 was never understood to be a reference to the Messiah, even though any Christian reading the passage cannot help but think of Jesus. We must also recognize that we have something to learn from the Jewish emphasis on ethical behavior in this life, our obedience to God being a requirement whether there is an eternal reward for it or not. Even among those traditional Jews who believe in an afterlife, the afterlife is not the emphasis. Obedience to the will of God now is what matters, and the healing of this wounded world is our obligation.

Islam

Archbishop Anastasios has said that we are closer to Islam than to any other non-Christian religion because Muslims also revere Christ and believe in his birth to the Virgin Mary. Some Christians object to this on the grounds that unlike the Jews, whose prophets were real, Muhammad was a false prophet and Islam is a regression. This is hardly the way to begin a dialogue with those who sincerely believe that the Koran was dictated by an angel and speaks directly of God, clearing away the misunderstandings into which Jews and Christians have fallen. This is where the Muslim begins, as well as with the belief that submission to God's will matters more than anything else. *Islam* means "submission" and the Muslim is "the one who submits."

The life of Charles de Foucauld is instructive here. He was a rather dissolute young man, expelled from the French army for immorality, who took on some spy work for France in North Africa, where he encountered Islam. He had long since abandoned the Catholicism of his childhood, but when he saw the fervent and frequent prayers of Muslims, he began to reconsider his relationship to God. He admired Islam but returned to a fervent practice of Catholicism, tried the monastic life and found the Trappists too soft, and ended his life as a hermit in North Africa, admired by many of the surrounding Muslims for his obvious prayerfulness and ascetic life. Sadly, he was eventually murdered by bandits. Many Catholics consider him a martyr and a saint.

What is interesting is that his return to Christian faith began with an encounter with Islam. There he saw a religion that informed the whole of life. The sense that prayer is a daily and frequent obligation, that charity is essential, that our behavior must always be informed by a sense that we must be obedient to God's will for humanity is considered by some in the West to be fanatical. Those Muslims who feel threatened by some aspects of Western culture—decadent sexuality, materialism, taking the relationship with God lightly—are right to feel threatened. Some of their negative judgments are in fact correct.

The method praised by Archbishop Anastasios in some earlier Orthodox-Muslim encounters seems still to be best: see what we have in common and begin there, while rejecting the idea that the Trinity is a repudiation of monotheism. We must also understand that the Muslims share the Jewish dismay at what Christians say about Jesus' incarnation. Muslims revere Jesus as a prophet and even celebrate Mary's virginity but cannot accept the idea that a prophet of God should come to such a scandalous end as death on a cross. This seems blasphemous, a reduction of God's nature to the limitations of humanity. This encounter with the amazement of others can be a bracing shock for us: it can show us exactly how startling the Christian claim is and may surprise us into a new appreciation of our faith.

Hinduism

Hinduism is so varied in its manifestations that it is impossible to speak of an encounter with Hinduism in the same way as we speak of encountering Judaism or Islam. There is no single Hindu doctrinal system, and some Hindus would argue that Hinduism is monotheistic, while others would not. But if you look at the scriptures that Hindus revere, especially the Bhagavad-Gita and the Upanishads, you will find some things that can engage Christians. The Upanishads express a devotion and sense of praise that is close to Christian sensibilities, and there is even an incarnation doctrine of sorts in the Bhagavad-Gita, where the Krishna, seen first in human form, displays his divine self to Arjuna.

In addition, where there is a kind of incarnation in Hinduism, it is God *disguised* as human—not God as fully human while at the same time fully divine. While divinity is necessary to maintain or restore order in Hinduism, the belief that God redeems a wounded world is absent.

One aspect of Hinduism has been a major contributor to New Age thought in an attenuated way. That is the belief that every human being shares in the divine nature, and the purpose of religious striving is to uncover the divinity within. However much this might look, superficially, like the Orthodox idea of deification or *theosis,* there is an essential, crucial difference. In Hinduism (and by extension, its New Age offspring) the belief is that our divinity is ours by nature. In Orthodox Christianity we share God's life as God's gift to us, but as creatures, made from nothing by God, we are totally contingent on a God who is at once totally present and totally other. His gift to us of participation in divine life flows entirely from him, according to his free will; our nature is that of the creature, existing only because of God's will. So we are not divine by nature—indeed our own nature is so radically contingent that it is nearly nothing and would be nothing if God did not will us into being.

One aspect of Hinduism that might be instructive to Christians is the idea of life's stages: the student, the householder, the one who begins withdrawing from the world's attractions and obligations, and the final ascetic stage. The holiness we are called to can and does change with our time in life and its attendant obligations.

Buddhism

In some ways Buddhism, with its relative indifference to anything like our monotheistic idea of divinity, can seem so radically other, that a dialogue would appear to be impossible. But, some fruitful conversations have been held between Christian and Buddhist monks, and this may tell us where we can find the most valuable common ground. Paradoxically, it is on that common ground that we will also find what most divides us.

Buddhism can challenge us to see how lightly we usually use words such as "God" and "being" and "creation" and, especially, "self" or "soul." The idea that the soul is not a subsistent entity seems to contradict our most basic assumptions. If the self does not really exist, what is it that rises from the dead? It seems necessary for us to affirm that there is something God loves that is myself and yourself and that God means this self to be united with God's own life. At the same time, what I regard as my true self may in fact be false and illusory, not only because of sinful self-deception but also because when I attach my sense of self to a particular story or inner dialogue, I can go deeply astray. Is a person who has lost her memory to a stroke less herself? Is what God loves in us what we cherish in ourselves? It is interesting that many great writers on prayer, East and West, have mentioned the experience of the self as nothing when it meets God's presence. At the same time, we know from the Trinity that the self is always found most truly in a relationship of self-emptying love—even the Persons of the Trinity exist in relationship—and over a lifetime, one learns that it is in loving others, and in being loved, that the truest self emerges.

Perhaps the reason that monastic meetings between Christian monks and Buddhist monks have been fruitful is that those who spend a lot of time in prayer and meditation encounter the false moves the mind makes in the effort to protect the ego, and these take a common form. The resemblance between the Buddhist sense of mindfulness and the various ways the Orthodox *Philokalia* addresses the idea of guarding the heart are fascinating.

Both traditions caution against allowing either aversion or attraction to mislead us; both are careful and attentive about what might be called the psychology of prayer. At this level there can be fruitful discussion and learning on both sides.

What Dialogue Means

A Christian can learn much from dialogue with people from other religious traditions, but there are limits, and they involve both the respect we must have for the other's tradition and our own vocation as Christians. There is a tendency, especially in America, to downplay differences as if they were embarrassments and to emphasize those things in common. There is a seemingly opposite, but related, trend of celebrating *all* diversity as if it were good in and of itself to have a number of differing opinions, all understood to be equally valid and finally reconcilable. Emphasizing what we have in common is a good beginning point for inter-religious discussion, and even after we have identified those points on which we cannot agree, there are still fruitful areas of discussion and cooperation. But there are differences that may not be downplayed without betraying our own tradition, and in our attempts to seem companionable, we may be showing a lack of respect for the other's tradition.

One of the major differences between Christianity and Buddhism is the emphasis that the Christian tradition places on the idea of creation, of God as the sole creator, and of creation as something essentially good and wounded by sin. Buddhism posits a complex "independent co-arising" that involves a deep overlay of illusion, but the point is not the fulfillment of creation's goodness but being freed completely from the grip of the illusions to which *samsara* gives birth. The place of the self in Christian thought can be fruitfully challenged by an encounter with Buddhism; for example, we can be returned to the understanding that the true self—even within the Trinity—exists only in relationship and is never a monad, an isolate, individual unit. But, ultimately, we affirm the importance of God, of the otherness of God's divinity; we also affirm the goodness of the self loved by God and the hope, finally, that we will rise from the dead. The Buddhist who affirms the same thing must in the end become a Christian. The Christian who fails to affirm this will cease being a Christian.

This failure to affirm what makes us different as firmly as we affirm what unites us has led to some problems in Jewish-Christian dialogue. It has become almost a formula, in some circles, to move away from the painful past by suggesting that Jesus is the salvation for Christians but not of all people, thus avoiding the "supersessionist" claims that the validity of Judaism was completely cancelled by the coming of Christ. There are those who claim the Letter to the Romans in the New Testament implies an usurpation and absorption of the Jewish tradition by Christians, but there are others who read a continuing relevance of Judaism in its passages. Indeed, one can read Romans and the rest of the New Testament in a more complex way: the covenant with the Jews endures, and Christians have been grafted into it (see Romans 11) and should be grateful for that fact, but the Israel into which Christianity has been grafted has yet to be reconciled to its fullness in Christ.

In any case, a Christian must always proclaim that if Jesus is not the salvation of all, he is not the salvation of any. If a Christian,

Jew, Buddhist, Hindu, Muslim, Sikh, Animist, or agnostic makes it into the kingdom of heaven it will be because of what Jesus did on the cross. We may not agree with those who believe that everyone must consciously accept the truth of Christ's redemption or go to hell, but we really do have to insist that if they make it into the kingdom God willed for all from the beginning of time, it will be because of what the Father did in Jesus Christ. It will be the Holy Spirit working in their lives that leads them there, even though they may ultimately be surprised to find that out.

Georges Khodr believes that Western theology has somewhat confused the dialogue by an overemphasis on "salvation history," with its emphasis on God's self-revelation through history, culminating with Christ. Khodr, an Antiochian Orthodox metropolitan, writes:

> The economy of Christ cannot be reduced to its historical manifestation but indicates the fact that we are made participants in the very life of God himself. . . . The very notion of economy is a notion of mystery. To say mystery is to point to the strength that is breathing in the event. It also points to the freedom of God who in His work of providence and redemption is not tied down to any event. The Church is the instrument of the mystery of the salvation of the nations. It is the sign of God's love for all men. . . .Within the religions, its task is to reveal to the world of the religions the God who is hidden within it, in anticipation of the final concrete unfolding and manifestation of the mystery.[2]

[2]Georges Khodr, "Christianity in a Pluralistic World—The Economy of the Holy Spirit," *Ecumenical Review* 23 (1971): 123.

Our task in this dialogue must be approached with humility. We must be honest about the many ways in which Christianity has, in practice, violated its deepest commission, which is to manifest the compassion, the love, and the truth of Christ to a broken world. Khodr again writes: "A Christian community purified by the fire of the Spirit, holy unto God, poor for the sake of God, can in the weakness of the Gospel, take the risk of both giving and receiving with equal simplicity. It must accept the challenge as a brotherly admonition and be able to recognize, even in the guise of unbelief, a courageous rejection of lies which Christians have long been unwilling or unable to denounce."[3]

We cannot know what God wills for those who are not Christians. We do know that God has created all out of love and that God is merciful, and the fullness of the joy God wishes for all of us is beyond our imagining. We have to be careful, though: we must be prepared to be surprised at how little we know about what God wills for those of us who claim to be Christians. Even as we believe that Christianity is God's fullest and most profound revelation of the truth, and that Orthodoxy is its most thorough expression, we have to say this with some humility. We do not know and live out that fullness *ourselves*; each of us is capable of understanding only the most fragmentary and dim aspects of the truth we hope one day to encounter fully. Even if we are blessed enough to arrive at that day, if the vision of St Gregory of Nyssa is to be believed, it may only be the beginning.

We can conceive then of no limitation in an infinite nature; and that which is limitless cannot by its nature be

[3]Ibid., 127.

understood. And so every desire for the Beautiful which draws us on in this ascent is intensified by the soul's very progress towards it. And this is the real meaning of seeing God: never to have this desire satisfied.[4]

When Gregory speaks of "*every* desire for the Beautiful," we should look at the Orthodox theology of grace, which teaches that whatever we will be in eternity begins on this side of death; this is true for all human beings. Although this is not something that can be said to be "the Orthodox teaching," it may at least be a *theologumenon*—a teaching that one may believe, even if it is not Orthodox dogma—that the Buddhist who is moved to compassion by the teaching of the Buddha, or the Muslim whose charity is genuine, or the Jew whose reverence for the God of Israel is a transforming presence, or the Hindu whose devotion to Krishna is heartfelt, will be saved because in all of these movements of the soul and heart there are seeds of the Word. That Word, we must as Christians insist, is Jesus Christ, who alone is the salvation of human beings.

Given the riches we Orthodox Christians have, and despite how cold-hearted and unmoved by the gift we often are, it may be that, in the fullness of God's mercy, even we can be saved.

---

[4]H. Musurillo, ed., *From Glory to Glory* (Crestwood, NY: St Vladimir's Seminary Press, 1979), 147–148.

BIBLIOGRAPHY &
RECOMMENDED READING

This list includes some of the books consulted in the preparation of this work, as well as books that might interest readers wishing to explore the subject more deeply.

Ata'illah, Ibn. *The Book of Wisdom (Kitab al-Hakim)*. Victor Danner, trans. London: SPCK, 1971.

Bettenson, H., ed. *The Early Christian Fathers*. New York: Oxford University Press, 1987.

Conze, Edward. *Buddhism: Its Essence and Development*. New York: Harper, 1959.

Dawood, N. J., trans. *The Koran*. New York: Penguin, 1956.

de Bary, William Theodore, ed. *The Buddhist Tradition*. New York: Modern Library, 1969.

Denny, Frederick. *An Introduction to Islam*. New York: Macmillan, 1994.

Dupuis, Jacques. *Christianity and the Religions: From Confrontation to Dialogue*. Maryknoll, NY: Orbis Books, 2002.

Embree, Ainslie T., ed. *The Hindu Tradition*. New York: Modern Library, 1966.

Esposito, John. *Islam, the Straight Path*. New York: Oxford University Press, 1991.

Fackenheim, Emil. *Quest for Past and Future: Essays in Jewish Theology*. Bloomington, IN: Indiana University Press, 1968.

Griffiths, Paul. *An Apology for Apologetics*. Maryknoll, NY: Orbis Books, 1991.

_____, ed. *Christianity Through Non-Christian Eyes*. Maryknoll, NY: Orbis Books, 1990.

Haight, Roger. *Jesus, the Symbol of God*. Maryknoll, NY: Orbis Books, 1999.

Hardon, John A. *Religions of the World*. Westminster, MD: The Newman Press, 1963.

Hertzberg, Arthur, ed. *Judaism*. New York: George Braziller, 1961.

Hinnels, John R., ed. *The New Penguin Handbook of Living Religions*. London: Penguin, 1997.

Knitter, Paul F. *Introducing Theologies of Religions*. Maryknoll, NY: Orbis Books, 2002.

Lal, P., trans. *Dhammapada*. New York: Farrar Straus & Giroux, 1967.

Lindbeck, George. *The Nature of Doctrine: Religion and Theology in a Postliberal Age*. Philadelphia, PA: Westminster Press, 1984.

Lopez, Donald S., Jr., ed. *Asian Religions in Practice: An Introduction*. Princeton, NJ: Princeton University Press, 1999.

Marks, Barry A. *Judaism for the Non-Jew*. Springfield, IL: Templegate, 2003.

Prabhavananda, Swami, and Isherwood, Christopher, trans. *The Song of God: Bhagavad Gita*. Hollywood, CA: Vedanta Press, 1969.

Richardson, C. C., ed. *Early Christian Fathers*. New York: Collier, 1970.

Runciman, Stephen. *The Great Church in Captivity*. Cambridge: Cambridge University Press, 1968.

Schmemann, Alexander. *The Historical Road of Eastern Orthodoxy*. Crestwood, NY: St Vladimir's Seminary Press, 1977.

Smith, Huston. *The World's Religions*. San Francisco: Harper, 1958.

Smith, Jean, ed. *Radiant Mind: Essential Buddhist Teachings and Texts*. New York: Riverhead Books, 1999.

Smith, Wilfred Cantwell. *Islam in Modern History*. Princeton, NJ: Princeton University Press, 1997.

Stamoolis, James J. *Eastern Orthodox Mission Theology Today*. Maryknoll, NY: Orbis Books, 1986.

Tanakh: A New Translation of the Holy Scriptures. Philadelphia, PA: Jewish Publication Society, 1985.

Ward, Benedicta, ed. and trans. *The Desert Christian: The Sayings of the Desert Fathers.* New York: Macmillan, 1975.

Yannoulatos, Archbishop Anastasios. *Facing the World.* Crestwood, NY: St Vladimir's Seminary Press, 2003.

Zaehner, R. C., ed. *Encyclopedia of the World's Religions.* New York: Barnes & Noble, 1997.